Bethlehem's

Jerry G. Kaufman

ABSTRACT

This project is a regional case study of higher education institutions, employees, and students in the occupied Palestinian town of Bethlehem. A three-article format, this project employs autoethnography to explore the ways the author's religious community conceived of the holy land; mapping and photo documentation to explore the infrastructures of occupation surrounding Palestinian educational space; and interviews and direct observation to explore campus spaces, organizational issues, and pedagogical practices. In the autoethnography, the researcher uses reflective memory to reconstruct theologically and culturally rooted impressions of Israel and Palestine. The author also explores their later intellectual and social evolution away from Christian Zionism to a position that supports the Palestinian struggle for liberation.

In attending to the material conditions of the Israeli occupation, the study overlays ArcGIS spatial data from the United Nations with original maps of Palestinian educational spaces including campus locations, student markets, and commuting patterns. The resulting spatial representations are then used to explore notions of settler colonialism and spatial epistemology. The study finds that infrastructures of occupation impinge on Palestinian educational access, psychological readiness to learn, and natural knowledge building processes about place and land.

Exploring Palestinian educational spaces directly, the study draws on interview and focus group data with faculty, administrators, and students from three institutions of higher education in Bethlehem, Palestine. Participants were recruited using chain referral sampling for interviews that lasted between 60 and 90 minutes, exploring the daily practices, aspirations, and challenges participants face as educators or learners.

The study finds theoretical and practical implications. Curricular implications are suggested for Palestinian educators to include direct encounters with Palestine spaces unfamiliar to students. For foreigners, the study suggests responsible approaches to tourism and encounters that allow Palestinian stories about the land to be expressed. Finally, the study proposes the beginning of a framework for understanding epistemological functions of spatial encounters under settler colonial domination and a corresponding spatial pedagogy of liberation.

Keywords: higher education, Palestine, Bethlehem, settler colonialism, occupation, infrastructure, critical pedagogy

TABLE OF CONTENTS

List of Tables 24

List of Figures 25

Glossary 29

1. Introduction 34

    Research Design 37

        Reasons for the Study 40

        Questions 42

        Propositions 44

        Unit of Analysis 44

    Overview of the Dissertation 44

    Summary of Findings 47

        Convert to Critic: Autoethnography of a Former Christian Zionist 47

        Spatial Machinery: Settler Colonial Configurations and Epistemological Implications 48

        House of Bread: Palestinian Higher Education in Bethlehem 49

    Implications and Uses 50

    Publishing Plan 51

2. Convert to Critic: Autoethnography of a Former Christian Zionist 52

    Reflective Approach 54

    Soliloquy From a Christian Zionist Childhood 57

    Conversion and Post-Conversion 60

        Seeing Without Seeing 64

        Pilgrimage for a New Generation of Christian Zionists 65

    Christian Zionism as Theological Endorsement for Israeli Settler

        Colonialism 68

        Christian Zionism in the United States 68

        American Christians' Direct Support to Israeli Settlements 71

        What I Believe About Christian Zionist Theology 73

        Christian Zionism and Settler Colonialism 76

    Discussion 83

3. Spatial Machinery: Settler Colonial Configurations and Epistemological

    Implications 88

    Literature Review 90

        Spatial Production 91

        Settler Colonial Transfer 95

        Infrastructurespace 98

        Research Question 97

    Method 100

        Research Design 101

        Data Collection 102

  Data Analysis 103

  Role of the Researcher 104

Findings 106

  Roads and Tunnels 106

  The Separation Barrier (Also Known as the Apartheid Wall) 109

  Checkpoints 111

  Refugee Camps 113

  Surrounding Communities 116

  Campuses 118

  Spatial Locations and Educational Implications 120

  Checkpoints 127

Discussion 131

Spatio-Epistemics 132

4. House of Bread: Palestinian Higher Education in Bethlehem 137

Literature 139

  Present Higher Education System 139

  Post-Oslo Conditions 140

  Theoretical Grounding 142

  Research Questions 148

Methodology 149

  Case Study as Method 149

  Data Collection 150

  Data Analysis 154

Trustworthiness 155

Role of the Researcher 158

Findings 161

Profiles of Three Institutions 161

Theme 1: Challenges 169

Theme 2: Faculty and Administrator Aspirations for Students 173

Theme 3: Maneuvers to Overcome the Challenges 178

Profiles and Portraits 184

Discussion 188

5. Conclusion 191

Discussion 191

Spatial Machinery and Mind 192

Epistemological Resurgence 194

Implications 195

Revising Powerful Stories About Land 195

Reconfiguring Relationships to Space 197

Engaging With Leaders From Inside the Machinery 198

Parting Thoughts 199

CHAPTER 1

INTRODUCTION

I am conducting my PhD dissertation study on the higher education system in Bethlehem in the Occupied Palestinian Territory (OPT) of the West Bank. It is a qualitative case study about the ways Palestinian educators and learners navigate the physical and epistemological danger posed by the Israeli occupation as they pursue their educational goals. It is about faculty who teach, serve, and research; about students who commute, study, write papers, and socialize in the cafeteria; and about Palestinian colleges and universities and their operations as organizations. The larger socio-political context in which this system of Palestinian higher education operates is also in view: The Israeli occupation controls space, movement, and access throughout the Palestinian West Bank through mechanisms such as checkpoints, military deployment, tear gas, economic controls, and bureaucracy. This "matrix of control" (Halper, 2000, p. 1) impacts Palestinian higher education in countless complex ways. It affects how students select colleges to attend, and what kinds of commutes to expect; pedagogical options for faculty as they plan their syllabi; administrators who manage budgets and resource flows; and institutional access to supplies needed for pedagogical and organizational purposes. In addition to the occupation, this larger context in which higher education operates is characterized by the Israeli settlement project, which seeks to transfer Palestinians out of the center of life in Palestine. This transfer is both physical and epistemological and creates situations and discourses to which Palestinian higher education responds. The Oslo negotiation process in the 1990s also brought significant changes to the structure of the settler colonial project and the occupation. This study is finally about how

Palestinians respond to these challenges. It is about the choices students and their families make to go to college; about the daily commutes they make through checkpoints on their way to class; about faculty who strive to keep students connected to Palestine; and about the content they select, pedagogical approaches they take to help students grow in their Palestinian identity, and their capacity to live in a world of neoliberalism, occupation, and domination. From a theoretical perspective, this is a study of higher education under the physical and epistemological conditions of settler colonialism. Israel's settlement project and the attendant necropolitical occupation of Palestine are conditions under which generic approaches to teaching, researching, mentoring, and leading must be refashioned to perform functions they do not perform elsewhere. In addition to soldiers and weapons, settler colonial structures employ epistemological tactics to establish moral legitimacy (Veracini, 2010). Tactics include censorship, Orientalist discourses, silencing, and reframing identity. Likewise, Indigenous populations resist their oppression and colonization both through physical force and through epistemological processes such as storytelling, advocacy, writing, conversing, and teaching (Veracini, 2006, 2010). Higher education is a uniquely epistemological institution—it exists to generate and disseminate knowledge—so institutions of higher education play a significant role in this epistemological theater (Chatterjee & Maira, 2014; Clyne, 2019; Millican, 2018; Rhoads & Torres, 2006) which combines both struggle against and accommodation with settler colonial transfer.

Although scholars mark the outset of this settler colonial narrative differently, many would agree there were clear settler colonial structures in place by 1923, with the emerging British sponsorship of Jewish immigration and nurture of proto-state, Jewish institutions in Palestine (Gelvin, 2014; Khalidi, 2007). By the time Britain started moderating its actively Zionist policies in the 1930s, the Jewish community in Palestine had already organized intelligence and combat groups, deliberative bodies, and proto-governmental institutions: for example, the Haganah, the Jewish National Council, and the Histadrut all evolved in the 1920s. When the State of Israel was organized in 1948, these organizations became or helped found the Israeli Defense Force, the provisional government, and the national labor organization, respectively.

When the British withdrew from Palestine a few years after the second world war, the Jewish community declared the creation of the State of Israel and fought a war against Palestinian residents and neighboring Arab states. This war is the root of the present-day Palestinian refugee issue—when the war was over, the estimated 750,000 Palestinian civilians who fled were prevented from returning to their homes. Many of the descendants of these refugees still live in refugee camps throughout the Occupied Palestinian Territories (OPT; refers to Gaza and the West Bank) and neighboring countries. When this war was over, Jordan held what is now the West Bank and Egypt held Gaza. In the 1967 war, Israel defeated Egypt and Jordan, taking control of these areas. Israel has occupied these Palestinian areas since then.

Before 1967, Palestinians who pursued a higher degree generally did so in the Arab world or in the Soviet countries. A few studied in Europe or the United States (Baramki, 1987; Sullivan, 1991). After 1967, traveling for Palestinians became more complicated, creating internal markets for higher education in the recently occupied territories (Baramki, 1987; Sullivan, 1991). At least five universities opened in the 1970s to begin addressing this demand, and the Palestinian Council for Higher Education

(PCHE), the administrative body that governed these new institutions, was established at the beginning of the decade (Baramki, 1987). The PCHE was subsequently replaced by the Palestinian Ministry of Education and Higher Education (PMEHE) during the changes brought by the Oslo process in the early 1990s (RecoNow, 2016). The PMEHE was recently replaced by the Palestinian Ministry of Higher Education and Scientific Research in a move that separated tertiary from primary and secondary education and linked it to scientific research. Many Palestinian colleges and universities (PCUs) were secondary schools and academies until the Israeli occupation began, when their leadership responded to emerging local needs for tertiary options. Birzeit University, Bethlehem University, and An Najah National University are examples of secondary schools that moved into tertiary education in the 1970s (Baramki, 2010). Others were founded as colleges or universities from the outset starting in the 1970s, including Hebron Polytechnic University (1978), Islamic University of Gaza (1978), Al Azhar (1991), and Arab American University (2000). Al Quds University was formed through the merger of four independent colleges in and around Jerusalem in 1995, and Palestinians continue founding PCUs in the 2000s and 2010s, including Dar al-Kalima University of Arts.

Research Design

This study is an embedded, multiple case study design (Yin, 2017). The multiple cases aspect of the design means data were collected from multiple colleges and universities and kept separated into individual cases during case analysis before being compared across cases at the regional level. The embedded aspect of the design means there are two units of analysis within each case: individual students, faculty, and administrators serve as one level of analysis and the institution itself, its policies, character, practices, and physical location serves as a second level of analysis. By conducting the research in this way, sufficient specification allows the exploration of different kinds of research questions.

Some of the most helpful case studies in social science are those that explore a *critical case* (Flyvbjerg, 2006). Although the execution of methods remains very important, the larger value of a case study arises from the strategic selection of the phenomenon that will be studied. For example, cases in which the conditions are favorable for a certain hypothesis to take place can revolutionize understanding if under those conditions the hypothesis is falsified. Such would be a critical case. This study on higher education in Palestine is such a critical case in a few ways. Westerners, maybe Americans in particular, are fitted with Orientalist (Said, 1978) lenses—representations of "the East" or "the Arab"—that distort our understanding of Palestine and Palestinians. Case study accepts a level of detail that can falsify the implicit orientalist hypotheses with which we read the news. Given the extreme conditions within which Palestinian higher education operates (occupation, settler colonialism), capacities and achievements successfully practiced under those conditions could possibly be affirmed for contexts with less acute challenges.

As a case study, this research is not intended to be generalizable in any statistically validated sense to other contexts, but rather, generalizable to theoretical propositions (Yin, 2017). The case is intended to provide theoretically stimulating insight into higher education and settler colonialism, social epistemology, and spatial construction. It is not that certain observations from the case are completely dissimilar to forms in other settings, but that similarities or differences cannot be taken for granted. Thus, this study seeks not to generalize to a population, but to generate a study that is available to individual scholars, practitioners, and interested parties who can recognize similarities and do their own work of appropriation, translation, and comparison, what Flyvbjerg (2006) called *transferability*.

I began work on this dissertation in 2019, months before the world started hearing headlines from Wuhan and then locked down soon thereafter. This timing was fateful and made an impact on the whole project—I made it in person to Bethlehem that year, but then could not visit again until spring of 2022, only months before I finished the dissertation. Of the 42 official interviews and countless other conversations I have had with Palestinian professors, administrators, and students, perhaps half were done in person, during one of my visits. The other half were done between 2019 and 2022 on Zoom, usually in the early hours in my time zone to catch my participants in the mid-afternoon Jerusalem time.

I started the project with assumptions that I have now set aside. I thought all of my participants would see their work in terms of resistance to the Israeli occupation and settler colonial project—although it is not my place to say now whether that assumption is true, I have noticed that some Palestinian scholars make assessments about *each other* regarding their relative positions *vis a vis* the occupier. I learned many other things as well. It is due to this dynamism, this evolutionary character, that I allowed the research design to emerge over time—I could not possibly have known all I needed to know at the outset of the project to ask exactly and all the right questions at that time. As I learned, my insights developed and gave rise to new questions. A few of these questions developed into major areas of interest and incubated questions I adopted as formal research questions. Chapters 2 and 3 both emerged in this way.

Reasons for the Study

I had many reasons for studying Palestine, some academic and some personal. Academically, I see much of the existing higher education scholarship and practice as culturally limited—it is produced in and indexed to "the west," and as such, it is built on social, political, and economic assumptions that cannot be taken for granted in other geographies. Given the globalization of western educational structures, even the research produced in other parts of the world is still often referenced to globalized American and European norms. Assumptions such as stable political regimes, national sovereignty, reasonable assumption of physical safety, and freedom of movement are all fundamentally assumed in the places where higher education research is produced. I wanted, with this dissertation, to explore higher education in a context where many of these assumptions must be encountered not as assumptions but as variables. I also selected this topic because it offered the chance to explore connections between physical space and knowledge production. In reading social theory about the construction of space and critical geographers, I find it persuasive that spatial configurations and conceptions play a much larger role in shaping social norms and prospects for knowledge production than might be assumed if space were just a neutral container for human action. Because space is configured (by groups with the power to do so), it differentiates between communities based on location and spatial status. These differentiations have implications for knowledge prospects across zones, borders, and geographies.

I also wanted this dissertation to be an opportunity for reflection on my own social, theological, and physical world. I selected this topic so I could reflect briefly (in Chapter 2) on the ideological role of my theological community in world affairs. I wanted to trace the Christian Zionism of my religious community downstream to the places and people affected by them. To even begin down this path, I had to accept that my theological beliefs have implications for other people. In that sense, my beliefs are not private—they have public meaning and implications. What seems plausible, what I hear and accept, what I do and say with what I believe in Chicago, IL, flows to other parts of the world and makes life easier for some and harder for others. It starts with recognizing I am implicated in a small but real way in the fate and affairs of people I do not know, but who serve as characters in my theological narratives. Palestinians did not ask to be characters in my church's theology, and the fact that they are has done them harm. The Christian Zionism that is a stream within my broad, church background carries implications for the lives of real people. Because my ideas are consequential for others, they should be approached with care and responsibility and an ethical framework that goes far beyond academic freedom or freedom of conscience. This dissertation is my attempt to approach a community that has historically been rendered invisible or framed as dangerous by my society. I want to make my own contributions to truth telling, which I see as a condition of justice and justice—at least a certain kind of justice—as a condition for true peace.

This study has also been a chance to problematize my worldview in ways I need. I see myself as an inheritor of a past and participant in a present settler colonial context. I am a White American with northern European lineage. As such, I am a beneficiary of the colonization of North America, the establishment of the United States, and the transfer of this ground from Native communities to the United States government. Indeed, my wife and I own a piece of that land. As this characteristic of my identity becomes clearer to me, I want to be more self-aware of my own social position and ready to learn from others, especially from people who live under oppression. To that point, this study gave me the chance to hear from higher education colleagues and students who seek to teach and learn under a military occupation that facilitates a colonization project. This is not merely important academically, but to my personal and epistemological life.

Questions

I started this study with a few questions to guide the initial phases of the project. As the study progressed, I added additional questions and modified existing questions. What priorities are prominent among faculty, administrators, and students in the Palestinian higher education system? How do Palestinian colleges encounter structures of the occupation at institutional and individual levels? How do Palestinian faculty, administrators, and students interpret their encounters with the Israeli occupation and settlement project as they pursue their priorities? How do Palestinian students, faculty, and administrators narrate the relationships between the Israeli occupation and settlement project, Palestinian higher education, and Palestinian national outcomes? How do Palestinian higher education agents resist the structures and effects of the Israeli occupation and settlement project in pursuing their priorities? What are the main features and salient aspects of the space within which higher education space is situated? How are higher education spaces configured? How do nearby spatial configurations of occupation and transfer influence prospects for Palestinian knowledge production in general and education more specifically? How has my own religious background influenced the ways I approach this study? Using these initial questions, I generated a more formal set of research questions:

> RQ1: How do faculty and administrators working at Palestinian colleges and universities perceive the occupation to affect their students, their institutions, and their work?
>
> RQ2: How do faculty and administrators working at Palestinian colleges and universities describe their efforts to create and sustain meaningful educational opportunities for students and pursue their research, given the unique challenges of life in occupied Palestine?
>
> RQ3: What physical and social conditions do students, faculty, and administrators experience as they navigate structures of the occupation in pursuit of education and research goals?
>
> RQ4: How do students at Palestinian colleges and universities narrate their life experiences and goals?

The case study methodology used for this project allowed the use of various data types to pursue findings to each of these questions. Interviewing individuals gave me insight into the questions about perceptions, priorities, and values. Mapping offered opportunities to explore the questions about space and geography. And direct observation offered insight into the question about educational spaces. Autoethnography gave me ways to explore the question about my religious background.

Propositions

I had several propositions with which I designed the study, propositions that provided a rough approximation of working assumptions and hypotheses. Propositions included: (a) The Israeli settlement project and associated occupation hinder, pressurize, and impinge upon Palestinian higher education. (b) Palestinian educators and students navigate the physical infrastructures of occupation and their associated bureaucracies in ways that influence educational structures. (c) The higher education system resists the structures and effects of the Israeli occupation and settlement project. (d) The Palestinian higher education system advances a complex set of priorities in relationship to national aspirations, connection to the land, connection to global community, and access to resources. (e) Palestine operates as a complex set of symbols in the American evangelical imagination characterized by Islam, terrorism, and irrationality.

Unit of Analysis

As a regional case study, Palestinian higher education supplies multiple options for units of study and levels of analysis. As an embedded case study, the project utilizes both individuals and institutions as units of analysis. As an autoethnography, Chapter 2 utilizes personal memories and discourses as units of analysis. Chapter 3 works with spaces, locations, and infrastructures using maps as a medium and interview data as a source of narrative about these spatial structures. Chapter 4 works with institutions and individuals as units of analysis.

Overview of the Dissertation

In Chapter 1 (the present chapter), the overall topic is introduced (higher education in Bethlehem, Palestine); the research design is presented, including reasons for the study, questions, propositions, and units of analysis; a summary of findings is offered; and a note is made about publishing options. What does a member of a faith community characterized by Christian Zionism bring to a study about Palestine? In Chapter 2, I developed reflexive journals from the dissertation process into an autoethnographic exploration of the implicit Christian Zionism of my background and my path to my current, critical evaluation of that Christian Zionism. This article also uses documents from two Christian Zionist organizations and applies critical discourse analysis to identify absences, obfuscations, and maneuvers in the writings. To engage with an academic articulation, I also briefly discuss a small group of scholars seeking to develop what they call the *New Christian Zionism*. The article concludes with an essay exploring resonances between Christian Zionist tropes and settler colonial tactics of transfer. The study ends with evidence that Christian Zionism, at least in some versions, seeks to provide theological warrant for settler colonial transfer of land and populations in Palestine.

How do Israeli-built infrastructures and policies of occupation and transfer influence prospects for Palestinian knowledge production in general and education more specifically? Chapter 3 is a geo-spatial case study of Bethlehem in the Palestinian West Bank, maps infrastructures that inscribe occupation and population transfer into the landscape, and uses these maps as a basis for reflection on the implications of the emergent physical landscape on prospects for knowledge production within Palestine. Using GIS maps and layers from UN OCHA, I overlaid infrastructures with spaces in and around Bethlehem, including residential space, commercial space, and educational space. Spatial data is layered into GIS maps and analyzed for proximities between Palestinian higher education space and occupation infrastructures. This data is assembled into multiple spatial profiles that map the configurations of infrastructures, institutions, people, and resources in multiple exemplar enclaves in the West Bank. Interview and documentary data that correspond to these proximities are triangulated to generate deeper understanding about the impacts of these proximities on higher education functions. Reviewing various combinations of layers and shifting focus to multiple sections of the map prompted further questions and reflections about the overlaps and disjunctures between the physical landscape and Palestinian knowledge ecology. I also used interviews with Palestinian faculty and administrators at colleges in Bethlehem who shared their perspectives and experiences of various physical features in and around Bethlehem. The study suggested physical relationships that may influence knowledge and education prospects and provided a basis for the development of a series of conceptual schematics to depict these ideas. They are not positive proofs or laws, but rather a series of frameworks designed to prompt further questioning about the epistemological and educational dispositions of occupation-related infrastructure in Bethlehem.

The Israeli occupation presses against Palestinian student life and learning in various ways, prompting Palestinian educators and students to respond as they pursue their goals. Chapter 4 draws together interviews, documents, and direct observations to describe these pressures, aspirations, and responses among Palestinian administrators and faculty. This chapter focuses on higher education in the Bethlehem region. Palestinian educators described a range of challenges produced by the Israeli occupation and the unique pressures they create for Palestinian students, educators, and higher education institutions. They also described the educational aspirations and goals they have for their students and the ways they and their students navigate the challenges as they pursue these goals. The article concludes with a discussion about the implications of this case for broader understandings about knowledge production in settler colonial contexts. Chapter 5 offers an expanded summary of findings across the study and explores implications of the study for settler colonial theory, spatial theory, and higher education frameworks. It also includes discussion of something I am calling epistemological resilience and final comments.

Summary of Findings

As separate embedded studies, each chapter presents different sets of findings in detail. To offer an overview, this section develops a summary of the overall findings. Readers can refer to each chapter for more detailed findings, methods, and supporting evidence.

Convert to Critic: Autoethnography of a Former Christian Zionist

My religious community regularly tells theologically framed stories about the *holy land*. Although these stories are enmeshed with scriptural and doctrinal interpretations about land, history, and eschatology (doctrine about what will happen at the world-historical level in the future), they are enmeshed in a Christian Zionist worldview that can be discerned in my religious community. As a United States citizen and a member of a particular expression of Christian practice, the pro-Israeli sentiments of my community emerge at the intersection of both identities. In my community, the analogue to these sentiments has been a corresponding lack of knowledge and attention to Palestine and Palestinians. Thus, theological energy both raises Israeli prominence and status and obscures or even degrades Palestinian narratives. In analyzing communication from selected contemporary Christian Zionist organizations, similarities between Christian Zionist arguments and settler colonial discourses of Indigenous population transfer. This article concludes that Christian Zionism, in certain expressions, can resonate with settler colonial initiatives at best and actively abet settler colonial rhetoric at worst.

Spatial Machinery: Settler Colonial Configurations and Epistemological Implications

Higher education space in Bethlehem is in a spatial matrix of occupation- and settlement-related infrastructures. Campuses are proximate to a separation barrier and a checkpoint that are part of this occupation. All campuses are proximate to urban refugee camps. These infrastructures can be sites of clashes, protests, and violence. These clashes can expand at times to border or even breach campus spaces. Even when there are no clashes, these are sites of daily monotony, dehumanization, and degradation. Some of the students enrolled at Bethlehem institutions live in East Jerusalem, so they must pass through the checkpoint any time they have classes or meetings. Some enrolled students have refugee status and live in the refugee camps. These students move in and out of different kinds of spaces where demands on them shift from space to space. In this context, campuses are constructed with walls and guarded gates to help control who accesses campus. They also seek to provide quiet spaces, spaces for socialization, study space, space for eating, classroom space, office spaces, lab spaces, studio spaces, and other configurations of space that facilitate learning.

House of Bread: Palestinian Higher Education in Bethlehem

Given the instability and danger of living in the West Bank, Palestinian faculty and staff are concerned about their students' physical, mental, and spiritual safety. They are aware their students experience stress navigating life under the Israeli occupation which includes passing the checkpoints, not being able to leave the West Bank for the most part, facing bleak employment prospects, losing friends or family to violence or imprisonment, and a shrinking access to rural and natural space. Faculty also see that their students would like to leave the West Bank if possible and establish their lives elsewhere. Given these challenges, faculty and administrators seek to make their campuses places of physical safety and when this is not possible, to close campus or to move classes to other areas such as local church buildings.

Given these primary findings, this study concludes the physical conditions and policies of occupation and settlement colonialism function as an epistemological environment upon which Palestinian knowledge (and not only Palestinian bodies) is impinged. Spatial control limits the knowledge producing power of direct encounters in areas that are restricted. Relatedly, the reduced engagement between Palestinians from different parts of Palestine that results from demobilization reduces the knowledge-producing effects of social encounters. In this context, Palestinian higher education in Bethlehem responds to the epistemological control on many levels and in many ways. Faculty provide students the opportunity to encounter Area C and Palestinian students from other parts of the West Bank. Institutions seek ways for students to practice core skills, even when necessary resources are scarce or restricted.

Implications and Uses

The dissertation is suggestive of a range of implications and uses across different audiences. First, much of the higher education literature is Euro-American-centric and takes regional political and social norms for granted, norms such as political stability, freedom of movement across internal borders, and institutional resourcing. As a contribution to this literature, this case is a potent challenge to many of these norms and has the potential to helpfully problematize frameworks and best practices that take these norms for granted. How, for example, does a shift into the Palestinian context destabilize notions about student success, diversity, pedagogy, and governance in higher education? Thinking now about the critical scholars, how might this case enrich the discussions about anti-coloniality and de-coloniality in higher education around the world?

Second, scholars of settler colonial theory may find value in how this case asks settler colonial questions of higher education. Much of the scholarship is pitched in a larger social scope or in political or community contexts, so the application to a particular sector offers a potentially distinctive angle. By posing these questions of higher education and interrogating the physical landscape, this case opens opportunities for settler colonial scholars to think about connections between spatial control and prospects for knowledge production, knowledge keeping, and other epistemological functions in Indigenous society. Scholars of higher education may also find ideas such as adaptive pedagogies and infrastructurespace to stimulate new questions for their work.

Third, as a contribution to Palestinian studies, this case offers a unique application of ongoing work on Palestine as a settler colonial subject and on higher education. There may be value in the connections drawn between the case and notions proposed in this study, such as spatial-epistemology, de-colonialism in higher education, and transnational stories about land.

Forth, Palestinian educators were among the principal participants in this study. I hope they will also benefit from it. Although I may not be able to fully articulate the specific ways this project will be beneficial, I have noticed among some educators a curiosity around some of the theoretical resources employed in the study, especially the idea of decolonizing assemblages from la paperson (2017). Perhaps by pointing to these ideas, this case can prompt a deeper dive into the mechanics of building resurgent pedagogies on the model of these assemblages. I also hope, through this case, to remind the rest of the academic world of our Palestinian colleagues—they are engaged in deep and important work and should be on our minds, in our collaborations, and connected to our discussions. Otherwise, we all miss out.

Publishing Plan

The articles in this study have not been published elsewhere. I intend to continue developing the research trajectories initiated in this dissertation and turn the dissertation into a book project. I plan to seek an academic press with a record of publishing on topics related to Palestine such as Routledge, University of California, Palgrave Macmillan, Stanford, or MIT. Alternatively, Christian presses such as InterVarsity Press or Eerdmans may present an opportunity to address these thoughts to evangelicals.

CHAPTER 2

CONVERT TO CRITIC: AUTOETHNOGRAPHY
OF A FORMER CHRISTIAN ZIONIST

Studying Palestine responsibly is complicated. To prepare for my dissertation study, I reflected about my role as a researcher and how I was socialized to relate to the idea of Palestine. I am a White Protestant from the Upper Midwest of the United States, which means my ideas about Israel and Palestine arose from religious, political, and cultural contexts. I grew up with vivid ideas about ancient Israel (through Bible stories) and some awareness of modern Israel (mostly through the news), but I was largely unaware of Palestine and Palestinians. This self-reflective process gave me the chance to explore my own assumptions, values, and beliefs and how they are shaping this study. My reflections coalesced around Christian Zionism, a theological ideology that is part of my religious background and identity formation. Theologically, Christian Zionism is the conviction that the creation of the modern state of Israel fulfills Biblical prophecy (McDermott, 2016). Socially and historically, this conviction corresponds to the Christian Zionist movement which is an "organized political and religious effort to support the state of Israel" (Hummel, 2019, p. 1). Smith's (2013) formulation of Christian Zionism brings these ideas together: Christian Zionism is "political action, informed by specifically Christian commitments" that seeks to "preserve Jewish control over the geographic area now comprising Israel and Palestine" (p. 2).

My purpose for these autoethnographic reflections is twofold. First, I explore how I, as the instrument of research, affect my process and conclusions. I am the carrier of assumptions, ideologies, and interests that should be surfaced and disclosed to whatever degree is possible. I present reflections about my conversion away from Christian Zionist constructions in my theology. It would be disingenuous to imply I ever was an active Christian Zionist. Israel was rarely salient in my community, so my Christian Zionist perspectives were largely a latent acceptance of ideas from my social context. Yet, it would also be disingenuous to suggest that Christian Zionist ideas or sentiments do not still influence my perspective in subtle or unconscious ways. One of the purposes of the self-reflection in this article is to review this ideological residue.

Second, I identify and seek to untangle and evaluate ideologies and identities in which I am deeply socialized but that pose a threat to my credibility as a researcher and the validity of my study. Recognizing Christian Zionism as containing political aims points to a recognition that theology is constructed in social, cultural, national, racial, and other contexts that can influence the inclusion, emphasis, and relations of theological points. Theology can be constructed in pursuit of a variety of social or political aims, such as racial subjugation (Carter, 2008; Jennings, 2010; Noll, 2006), nationalism (Robbins & Crockett, 2018) and settler colonialism (Cherry, 1972). As a result, theology can be analyzed discursively, and I perform such an analysis in the second half of this chapter. As a higher education professional and scholar at a faith-based institution, I am also interested in ideological links between religious instruction in higher education in the United States and Israel, and I draw some of these links into the analysis.

Among those who read this chapter, I hope to attract some Christian Zionists. To readers who fit that description, I want to say my path away from Christian Zionism was slow and involved intuitive discomfort with hermeneutics and implications, and as you will see, with the inability of Christian Zionism to provide an adequate basis for engaging with *all* the people of the holy land. Although I now hold a different ideological position, I hope to remain in serious and loving conversation with you. Some may feel the focus of this dissertation to be biased by not representing more pro-Israeli perspectives or by being what Christian Zionists call supersessionist, to which I will offer a few rebuttals. First, the scope of the dissertation is about Palestinian higher education and my relationship to the topic—it does not encompass the whole so-called Israel/ Palestine conflict; thus, fully representing pro-Israeli arguments is not in the scope of the dissertation. Second, Israeli and Christian Zionist perspectives are familiar within my religious community, and I choose to frame my dissertation as an exploration of voices and perspectives that have historically been theologically and socially invisible in that same community. Third, I encourage readers to engage with what I have written, not with what I have not written—they should not take silence on topics about which they might want me to have written to imply that I do not think these issues are important or that I take a particular position about them.

Throughout the study, I tinkered with the question of the relationship between myself and my project—what does it mean for a Protestant from Illinois to study higher education in Palestine? Slightly reframed, my research questions for this chapter are: (RQ1) What does a member of a faith community shaped by Christian Zionism bring to a study about Palestine? (RQ2) How do I now evaluate Christian Zionism?

Reflective Approach

To address the first research question, I reflected on personal memories about Israel and Palestine and the interpretation of these encounters offered by my religious context. Luttrell (2010) outlined a model for qualitative research design that places reflexivity at the center. Questions such as how researchers are "part of the setting, context, and social phenomenon" (p. 161) they are studying and how researchers will *name* themselves to participants and readers move to the center. I appreciate this perspective and seek to enact ongoing reflexive practices throughout this study. I include in the narrative diagnostic events that served as benchmark moments in the formation of my perspectives on Israel/Palestine. Earlier memories connect to Christian Zionist perspectives, and later memories connect to my intellectual journey away from Christian Zionism and my unfolding perspectives. I used these reflections as the basis for a soliloquy with which I open the article. This soliloquy partakes of what Saldaña (2015) discussed as monologic thinking, which offers "windows into the person's private mind—her or his values, attitudes, beliefs, emotions, and experiences" (p. 173). Although Saldaña's discussion was about allowing participants to monologue, I found the opportunity to reflect and write about my memories and beliefs provided a window for me into my own mind and access to new insights about my subjectivities.

I also wrote reflexive memos to record reflections about my assumptions, values, and beliefs as they surfaced during my research. I gathered relevant memos and treated these as primary data for an auto-ethnographic-like analysis. Autoethnography "blends case study intimacy with ethnographic cultural revelation" (Saldaña, 2015, p. 159). Autoethnography is not merely about self-narrative—it is the *use* of self-narrative to gain more intimate and concrete access to the culture in which the author participates. I found it helpful to think of autoethnography as having three defining features: Autoethnography (a) includes a systematic process of collecting data, (b) draws on the personal experiences of the author/researcher as part of the data set, and (c) aims at increased cultural understanding through analysis (Chang, 2016). Through systematic recollection and analysis (first feature) of personal experiences of Christian Zionism in my childhood and early adulthood (second feature), I aimed to describe the links between conservative American Protestantism and Israel/Palestine (third feature). Based on the poles of autoethnography—self and culture—I enriched my memos by conducting additional research to connect my individual experiences to broader Christian Zionist expressions of conservative Protestantism in America.

To address the second research question, I used two approaches. First, I re-read relevant books and passages from the Bible including the first five books of the Bible (Jews refer to them as the Torah), Daniel, the Gospels, and Revelation. I also read The New Christian Zionism (McDermott, 2016) and interacted with some of the main propositions of the approach. Second, I conducted a critical analysis of contemporary Christian Zionist texts, explored resonance between these texts, and documented settler colonial tropes in Israel/Palestine. I found two organizations that are part of the conservative American Christian world: Christian Friends of Israeli Communities (CFOIC) and Passages Israel, both of which I was already aware through faith-based connections. I signed up for a mailing list and received monthly newsletters from CFOIC for 12 months. I also obtained a tour book and map from Passages Israel that they give to Christian college students who go on their guided tours to Israel. I scanned these materials into qualitative data analysis software (Dedoose) and used the software to identify excerpts for analysis. I analyzed selected excerpts to explore the ways these discourses function to obfuscate and endorse Israeli settler colonialism. Although this analysis is not critical discourse analysis (CDA) per se, I borrowed features of CDA, such as "analysis of relations between discourse and other elements of the social process" (Fairclaugh, 2013, p. 10) and analysis that "addresses social wrongs in their discursive aspects" (Fairclaugh, 2013, p. 10). I include these analyses and argue that these Christian Zionist discourses offer theological cover for settler colonial discourses in the second half of the article.

Soliloquy From a Christian Zionist Childhood

One thousand paper cranes ascended into the air in the church multipurpose room. Each crane hung from its own fishing line connected at the top to concentric hoops and suspended from the ceiling. It was a handmade chandelier. I was in middle school in 1993 and 1994 when my Sunday School class folded origami cranes, a symbol of peace and good will. After folding cranes for a whole year, we strung them together into a massive handmade chandelier, a gift for Israel. We mailed it to the Israeli embassy in Washington, DC to celebrate the peace we heard they had achieved in the Oslo Accords with the Palestinians. To help us understand why this was significant, our Sunday School teacher played a documentary about Israel and the Palestinians—it left me with the impression that Israel had fought hard for its survival and then for peace. We believed Israel was God's chosen people and thought peace would mean an end to much Jewish suffering. As American Christians, we wanted to show our solidarity with Israel.

My religious community held mostly latent Christian Zionist beliefs throughout my childhood, and although these beliefs were relatively unimportant to me, they were real, nonetheless. It was a general belief I inherited from my church community, which was equally nominal in how they held onto their perspectives about Israel. We believed modern Israel was a fulfillment of prophecy, but we did not talk about it very often. If asked, I would have said Israel's creation was a fulfillment of prophecy, although I would not have been able to point to which prophecy or where it was in the Bible without a little time to do some research. I suspect it was the same for many of my peers—we believed Israel was our national ally, God's chosen people, and our religious kin, but our interest did not extend much further. It was a vague belief because it was basically irrelevant to us. It only became salient infrequently when Israel was in the news. Members of my family read Hal Lindsey's book, *The Late Great Planet Earth* in the early 1970s, a book that popularized the idea that the creation of the state of Israel initiated a cosmic countdown timer to the end of history (over 28 million copies since 1973). It was a wildly popular best seller when it came out and seems to have been indicative of my church's approach to Israel 20 years later.

At the same time, I did not know who the Palestinians were. All I vaguely knew was about a conflict between them and the Israelis. I have early impressions seeing the TV on in my grandparent's living room: I saw images of young adults and soldiers in the streets, young men throwing rocks, and soldiers and tanks returning fire with bullets and shells. These hazy memories were almost certainly news coverage of the first Palestinian Intifada in the late 1980s, broadcast into my grandparents' living room in Bloomington, MN. So, I saw Palestinians throwing stones in the street, but I did not understand what I was seeing, and given that I was more interested in toys and cartoons at the time, I did not give it much thought.

In my early teen years, my family had a box of Bible trivia cards. *What new names did God give to Abram and Sari? God called Abram Abraham and called Sari Sarah. How many books are in the Bible? There are 66 books in the Bible, 39 in the Old*

Testament and 27 in the New Testament. Most of the 39 books in the Old Testament are about Israel, how God called Abram and Sari to "go to a land that I will show you" (Genesis 12:1), how their descendants became a great nation, and how God was faithful to Israel. All of this spoke to me about the modern state of Israel too. I just assumed the Israel I saw on TV and the Israel from the Bible stories and trivia cards was the same Israel.

When I was a teenager, Tim LaHaye and Jerry Jenkins were writing best-selling adventure novels about the *end times*, a theological vision for what will happen at the end of history that comes from a particular interpretation of the Bible. The books (there are 12 books in the *Left Behind* series) presented a particular theological idea about what will happen at the end of earthly history: Christians suddenly disappear from the earth as they are miraculously transported to Heaven (the Rapture); an age of suffering and trials for those left behind (this term, *left behind*, is what the title of the series referred to) follows for 7 years (the Tribulation), and the armies of the earth wage a world-ending war (the Battle of Armageddon). The series presented Israel as a central, world-historical player in these events, although not always in a positive light. In the stories, Israel was left behind in the rapture because of their collective rejection of Jesus. In a later book in the series, 144,000 Jewish Israelis convert to Christianity and become passionate and effective evangelists of the Christian message. Much of the action occurs in Jerusalem. I read each book as it was released because I liked the fast-paced action, and I liked telling my family and friends about the story. I remember waiting impatiently for my turn on the library waiting list for each new title. I accepted these stories as presenting a dramatic interpretation of a vision that was theologically true about what would happen someday. And Israel figured into this vision as central to God's plans for the end times.

When terrorists flew the planes into the World Trade Center, it was devastating, but it also fit my worldview. I had embraced the impression, nurtured throughout my childhood, that aside from Israel, the rest of the countries and people in the Middle East were unstable and dangerous. I even had what I understood to be a Biblical explanation: As I understood it, from Genesis 17, the Arabs descended from Abraham's son, Ishmael, and Israel descended from Abraham's other son, Isaac. My professor hosted an FBI agent as a guest lecturer in class after the Twin Towers fell. His topic: Why Israel is a national ally. He said Israel is a force for good in the Middle East and also—he was speaking personally here—that Biblical prophecy showed that Israel is on the winning side of history, so the United States should be their ally. A couple months later, the first season of "24" aired, a new television show about an American agent pitted against global forces of terror. It was a popular American TV show about a counter-terrorist agent, Jack Bauer, that gave weekly expression to a wide range of stereotypes about people from around the world, particularly groups from the Middle East. These were easy stereotypes to accept at the time. After 9/11, the conceptualization of Israel came to signify something slightly different in my community than it had before—Israel was less connected to Biblical end-times prophecy in our minds and more connected to nationalistic fervor as an ally of the United States against terrorism.

Conversion and Post-Conversion

It was a story about a girl that first began to destabilize what I thought I understood about Israel. I heard a talk about Israel and Palestine at a conference. The speaker told a story about Bassam and his 10-year-old daughter, Abir (Figure 7). Abir was with her friends outside their school one day when an Israeli soldier fired a rubber-coated bullet from nearby. The soldier missed their target, and the bullet slammed into Abir's head. She died in the hospital a few days later. Since then, Bassam has been an activist for peace, seeking to end violence and achieve security and justice for his neighbors. The story gripped me, but it was not the tragedy or injustice of it that captured my attention, although both where true. What struck me was that it was a story about *particular Palestinians* who were *named*. I was 30, had been thinking about Israel from my earliest memories, and this was the first time I think I had ever heard a humanizing story about particular Palestinians—all previous references were collective and subject to

Figure 7

Aber Aramin, Soon Before She Was Killed

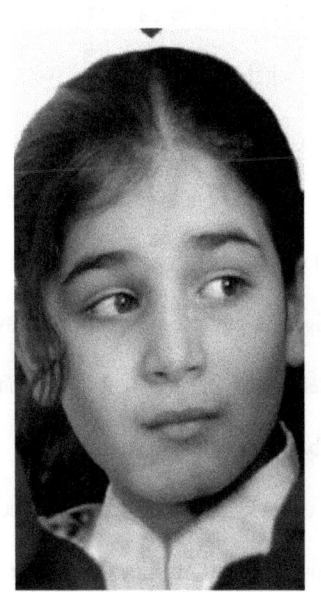

Credit: Courtesy of Bassam Aramin

what Memmi (1965) called the depersonalizing "mark of the plural" (p. 85). It unsettled me. I had sent 1,000 paper cranes to show solidarity. I had read books. I had theological explanations. But Bassam and Abir's story prompted me to reevaluate what I understood about Israel/Palestine. To be sure, a human story is not a panacea—but I was ready to hear it, and it became a turning point for my relating to Palestine.

I pursued opportunities to learn more. I began looking for opportunities to meet and interact with Palestinians. Daoud shared his family story with me. His family owns a farm near Bethlehem that has been in their family for years. It is located adjacent to expanding Israeli settlements. Settlers have harassed him and set fire to his orchards in efforts to scare him and his family away. In the following years, I read about Hanan Ashrawi (1995), Palestinian political leader and educator. I started reading Palestinian stories by Ghassan Kanafani, poetry by Mahmoud Darwish (1995), and scholarship by Edward Said (1978, 1994) and others. I read about 1948 and 1967, about the British Mandate, the Nakba, the creation of the state of Israel, the occupation of the West Bank and Gaza, and the unique challenges of those living in East Jerusalem. For me, these pieces, which so many dismiss as too complex to understand, tell a comprehensible story: It is a story, among other things, about settler colonialism. Settler colonialism can be understood as the systematic replacement of Indigenous groups with a settler society (Veracini 2010). Living in a settler colonial context as we do, Americans in the United States should be familiar with this concept (Dunbar-Ortiz, 2014; Keating, 2012)—although there are substantial historical differences, there are also similarities, especially at the level of tactics of displacement and land appropriation. After the Ottoman Empire dissolved during and after World War I, large areas in the Middle East were entrusted to the British, who promoted the creation of a Jewish state in historic Palestine. In 1948, that new state was established. But the land on which the state was founded was already inhabited by Palestinian populations who had been there for generations. Although both groups make conflicting land claims, the power differential between these groups is massive—the Israeli society and state possess the military and political power needed to transfer Israeli settlers into Palestine and transfer Palestinians to the social margins and physically into dense urban enclaves (Khalidi, 2020). These are the structural conditions that led to Abir's death. So, my slow conversion did not begin with a new Biblical interpretation or a sermon. It started with a story about a Palestinian father and daughter that was human enough to break through my theology. Where I used to see a theological story about the end-times, I now see a socio-political story about settler colonialism.

There are organizations currently engaging my students to proselytize them into Christian Zionist perspectives. Students at the college where I work have recently been traveling to Israel with a Christian organization that subsidizes their travel. Sitting with me over a cup of coffee when they get back, they tell me about their experiences. The overall social consciousness about Israel/Palestine has changed since I was in college—students today have access to information about Palestinians I did not have. And yet, they go to Israel and come back equally as unaware of Palestinian experiences as I was. This unsettles me because I have come to understand that what Americans think about Israel and Palestine has consequences for Israelis and Palestinians. Given the history of conservative evangelical support for Israeli settler colonial domination of the Palestinians, I see a problem there that I want to engage. So, although this is a story about my shift away from Christian Zionist ways of thinking about Israel/Palestine, I no doubt retain residual notions and sentiments. It is to these notions that I turn next.

Seeing Without Seeing

I described on the phone that I would like to study the ways the Israeli occupation impinges on Palestinian higher education. The first comment from one of my committee members upon hearing this idea: He asked me if Palestinians would be actors in the story I would tell, or only recipients of Israeli action. Would Palestinian initiative be part of the story? With that question, he revealed a flaw in my desire to study the Israeli occupation. In my concern about injustice, I wanted to study the initiator and maintainer of injustice. But the Palestinians have been resisting and criticizing the occupation for decades. I am not alone in my ignorance of the Palestinians—indeed, it can be argued that western social science is constructed to both see and unsee Indigenous groups (Smith, 2012). Many of the communities in my social world avoid the Palestinians. When possible, they subsume Palestinians into a larger category of Arabs, or else reframe them as international welfare recipients or terrorists. I had a video call with Amira (a pseudonym), a recent graduate from Birzeit University (north of Ramallah). An Israeli soldier had recently shot and killed a Birzeit student as he was participating in a protest. His body had been brought to campus, and hundreds of friends, family, and faculty gathered to pay their respects. I asked her about the meaning of the gathering. We looked at pictures of the event, mostly pictures of crowds around the body in an outdoor campus plaza. Amira pointed to the colors of the flags and their connections to political parties. She explained the objects that were placed around his body. There were flowers arranged to "dignify his body." There was a gun to "indicate that he resisted the occupation." The pictures could have been from CNN. I have seen images like them before—they looked like the news coverage I had seen in my grandparents' living room when I was 6 years old. But the cultural connotations American viewers took from the news coverage and those implied by Amira's explanation were starkly different. In the news, these images contribute to Western discourses about Palestinian tendencies to violence and revenge. As Amira explained the tenderness and mourning she saw in this gathering, I realized that *I can begin to have my eyes opened and still not understand*. This experience and others like it remind me that my incomplete knowledge entails epistemological responsibilities in my research to be culturally honest and self-critical, culturally humble, and ready for cultural learning. I see myself as accountable to Palestinians in these responsibilities, to help me proceed in ways that promote clarity around Palestinian experiences.

Pilgrimage for a New Generation of Christian Zionists

A few years ago, I started noticing that a lot of students at the college where I work were traveling to Israel. They came back from their trips talking about the meaningful experiences they had, which connected both to the historic and contemporary realities they found there. They visited Biblical sites like the Sea of Galilee and a traditional site for Jesus' baptism. They also met with Israeli civilians, political leaders, and military leaders to learn about modern Israel and the current political situation. The organization sponsoring these subsidized trips is called Passages Israel. It is connected to another organization called the Philos Project. According to the Passages website, these trips are designed for Christian college students to connect them to the "roots of their Biblical faith" as well as to the "modern-day miracle that is Israel." Student groups are recruited from college campuses, many of them faith-based institutions, and trips are subsidized—students might pay between $500–$1,000. According to the website (accessed in 2019), Passages has over 6,000 alumni of their trips from 157 colleges and other organizations.

One of the students at my college who went gave me his trip materials. They included a trip guide, a map, and other brochures and booklets. Glancing through these materials, it appears my student's group met with members of the American Israel Public Affairs Committee, Israeli politicians, journalists, and military officers. They also met with a couple of Palestinians, although the perspectives of these individuals do not seem to have been representative of most Palestinians in the occupied territories. In the manual, students are introduced to the places they will visit, each with a headline and a paragraph description. This section lists 10 sites of modern political interest, such as an Israeli settlement in the Palestinian West Bank they visited on the first day (Alfei Menashe), Independence Hall (where the Israeli Declaration of Independence was signed), and the Israeli Supreme Court. These places are interspersed with other locations that are more closely connected to Biblical history such as the Garden of Gethsemane (Matthew 26) and the Jordan River at one of the traditional locations for Jesus' baptism (Matthew 3). The mixture of these elements throughout the manual suggests a conflation between the "roots of our Biblical Faith" and the "modern-day miracle that is Israel" that would be difficult for a college student to untangle. The map my student received shows the whole region between the Mediterranean and the Jordan River (Figure 8). The political border between Israel and the Palestinian West Bank is present but hard to discern except for those who are looking for it. It is as if the map is making a contested political statement that the Palestinian West Bank is just a region in Israel. Larger Palestinian cities in the

Figure 8

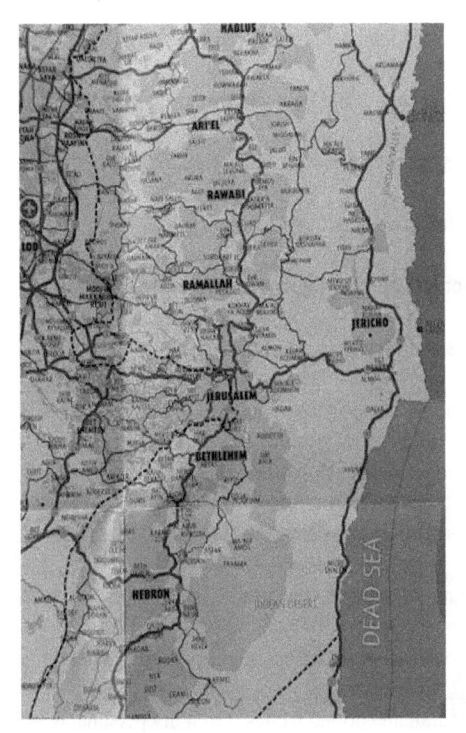

Map of Israel and the West Bank Provided to My Student on a Passages Trip

West Bank such as Jericho, Nablus, and Ramallah are labeled in bold black font, but the same font is also used for Israeli settlements such as Ari'el. There are dozens of smaller communities in the West Bank labelled in a smaller font. They include Palestinian towns like Bil'in and Nabi Saleh, but they also include, in identical formatting, Israeli settlements such as Alfe Menashe and Har Gillo. The West Bank is not labelled as such, replacing this term with ancient regional labels of Judea and Samaria. Again, the distinction between separate national spaces is suppressed by the design of the map. The map advances a certain Zionist ideology of the land as if it were a factual representation.

By now, dozens of the students at my college have attended these trips and used these materials.

So, I am still a member of Christian contexts where Christian Zionist ideas are promoted and make an impact. In the case of the Passages organization, the impact is among emerging adults whose ideas about Israel may be impressionable and who represent the next generation of Christians in the church.

Christian Zionism as Theological Endorsement for Israeli Settler Colonialism

Among conservative, American Protestants, adherence to Christian Zionism can regulate beliefs, practices, and policies of discrimination against and avoidance of Palestinians and Palestine. Israeli settler colonialism seeks to replace Palestinians as the most Indigenous and deserving claimant group to the land of Israel/Palestine. In the demographic and ideological war entailed in settler colonialism, settlement entities wield a variety of ideological, infrastructural, and armed tactics. From my personal experiences from the autoethnography and scholarship on settler colonialism and Christian Zionism, I argue in the second half of this chapter that conservative, U.S. Protestants can endorse, adopt, and theologize Israeli settler colonial claims in the context of Christian Zionism and that resulting belief systems inform political activism and influences policies and practices vis a vis the Middle East.

Christian Zionism in the United States

Bebbington (1989) suggested Euro-American evangelical Christians could be defined by four characteristic convictions: (a) belief in religious conversion, (b) a high regard for the Bible as God's revealed word, (c) the centrality of Jesus' death and resurrection to pay for the sins of humanity, and (d) the importance that Christians must share their faith with non-believers. More recently, Lifeway Christian Research (2015) and the National Association of evangelicals have used the following beliefs to identify evangelicals in national surveys: "The Bible is the highest authority for what I believe"; "It is very important for me personally to encourage non-Christians to trust Jesus Christ as their Savior"; "Jesus Christ's death on the cross is the only sacrifice that could remove the penalty of my sin"; "Only those who trust in Jesus Christ alone as their Savior receive God's free gift of eternal salvation."

Roughly three quarters of Americans identify as Christians (Pew Research Center, 2014). And almost one quarter of Americans identify themselves as evangelicals (Pew Research Center, 2014), making evangelicals the largest single category of Christians, larger than mainline Protestants, Catholics, Black Protestants, and other Christian groups. But evangelicalism is internally diverse, containing Pentecostal, dispensational, reformed, and other streams. Politically, evangelicalism has conservative, moderate, and progressive expressions as well. Not all evangelicals are Zionists (Burge, 2014), although since the 1967 war, Zionism moved into the conservative spaces in evangelicalism. To this conservative strain inside evangelicalism, names like James Dobson, Pat Robertson, Tim LaHaye, Jerry Falwell, Sr., John Hagee, and others have been household names. Having been raised in a conservative evangelical community, this is true of me, although now, I consider many of these figures "estranged members of the same family tree" (Burge, 2014, p. 177). These were conservative, White, male, evangelical, American leaders of the second half of the twentieth century and, in some cases, first decades of the twenty-first century. Many of them had their own organizational infrastructure, their own public platforms—radio shows, television shows, publishing houses, distribution networks, and so on, and made their way into elite political and cultural spaces (Lindsay, 2008). They commanded their own audiences, shaping both the ideological features and the political activism of White, conservative, American evangelicalism for decades. And many showed ongoing support for the state of Israel (Lewis, 2021; Sizer, 2004).

Christian Zionism was never merely generated by formal religious leadership—it was diffused and partially constituted in evangelical cultural influences as well, in artifacts such as films and books and in popular discourses. Picking up on this theme, Kaplan (2018) explicated the mythic romanticizing of Israel's founding expressed in Pat Boone's "The Exodus Song (This Land is Mine)" (1960). Pat Boone was an American celebrity and a self-professed evangelical. The song was the opening theme for *Exodus*, a popular film about the founding of Israel. I remember the novel from which the movie derives on a bookcase in the living room when I was growing up. Kaplan noted a variety of other Zionist artifacts with cache in the evangelical world, such as Hal Lindsey's (1971) *The Late Great Planet Earth* and Tim LaHaye's (1995) *Left Behind* series.

Although American evangelicals more broadly may be less actively engaged with Israel ideologically or in terms of activism than their leaders, they are almost certainly more engaged than their non-evangelical neighbors (Hummel, 2019). After all, the land where the modern state of Israel/Palestine is situated is the land of the Bible, and the Biblically-centered evangelical imagination maps resonates deeply with it—the Mount of Olives, the Mount of the Beatitudes, the Garden Tomb, Jacob's Well, the burial places of the Biblical Patriarchs, Mount Carmel, the place of the Last Supper, and Golgotha, to name only a few. American evangelicals tend to believe the modern, secular State of

Israel is the contemporary manifestation of Biblical Israel, investing it with theological and eschatological meaning (Hummel, 2019; Merkley, 2001).

American Christians' Direct Support to Israeli Settlements

After seeing social media posts from a Christian Zionist organization called Christian Friends of Israeli Communities (CFOIC) during the COVID lockdowns, I signed up for CFOIC's monthly newsletter and read each issue closely. CFOIC exists to enable "Christians to connect with the Jewish communities ("settlements") in the heart of Biblical Israel" (CFIOC website). I wanted to understand the CFOIC mission, values, and ways the organization used theology in its public communications. I received 13 monthly newsletters between March 2021 and March 2022. I uploaded these newsletters to a coding software and coded and analyzed text and images (see Appendix A for an example newsletter). The newsletters contain stories about Israeli "pioneers" living in settlements inside of the Palestinian West Bank, which CFOIC refers to by the ancient Israeli regional names: Judea and Samaria. There are more than 600,000 Israeli settlers across roughly 240 authorized and unauthorized settlements throughout the Palestinian West Bank (B'tselem, 2021). The stories frame settlers as heroic and virtuous, yet vulnerable, as they seek to enact *God's will* by fulfilling *Biblical prophecy* about Jewish return to Palestine while standing against hostile enemies.

The newsletters refer to Palestinians as Arabs in virtually every instance, thus *subverting the specific claims of Palestinians to Palestine*. In describing Palestinian resistance, the author uses emotive words such as *rampage* (June 2021 newsletter), *attack* (June 2021 newsletter), *riot* (June 2021 newsletter), *hostile Arab neighbors* (April 2021 newsletter) and *vile terrorists* (June 2021 newsletter). The corollary terms used to describe Israeli settlements include *isolated, threatened,* and *desperate* (April 2021 newsletter). The term "vast" is also used to construct the vulnerability of the "small" Israeli homes and the vast Arab town just beyond (June 2021 newsletter). The writer thus uses Orientalist discourses (Said, 1978) to present Palestinians as morally inferior and undifferentiated.

These newsletters also construct a *discourse about how Christians are natural friends of Israeli settlers*. Christian historic origins in Judaism are part of this, but the discourse also draws on shared belief in Biblical prophecy and a generalized appeal to common values and identity. From this shared religious identification, the newsletters contain multiple fundraising appeals each month. Some of the language uses Biblical/theological reasons to donate money for security and development projects in Israeli settlements. Bible verses are quoted throughout, in the body of the newsletter and in offset boxes. For example, under the slogan "Fulfill prophecy—plant a tree" and a call to donate money for planting trees in an Israeli settlement, the July 2021 newsletter quoted Ezekiel 36:8: "But you, O mountains of Israel, shall shoot forth your branches and yield your fruit to my people Israel, for they will soon come home." Some language uses humanitarian or security related reasoning such as protecting settlers from danger in their environment or providing educational programs for vulnerable populations in the settlements, such as children, those struggling with mental health, and orphans. The April 2021 newsletter reported that readers gave $1,500,000 to CFOIC for educational outreach and direct aid to Israeli settlements in the previous year. Based on other reports in the newsletters, settlements used these resources for community development and security equipment.

These newsletters all contain at least one opportunity for readers to contribute toward the development of natural landscapes in the settlements. For Father's Day, readers were invited to sponsor the planting of blueberry bushes in the settlements. For Mother's Day, readers could sponsor the planting of a tree. These sections of the newsletters are resonated with the research about how land management has been used to erase Palestinian connections to land as forests are planted over emptied Palestinian towns (Benvenisti, 2000; Khalidi, 2006). Who gets to plant and where plantings are made is political. It physically enacts one of the founding myths of Zionism that Jews made the dessert bloom (George, 1979). Indeed, the newsletter makes this connection explicit. "An area that was barren" in reference to the Palestinian West Bank, "with little infrastructure and almost no Jews, became a popular and beautiful place for Jewish families to raise their children in just over 40 years" (April 2021 newsletter).

The discourses about the vulnerability and virtue of Israel settlers and the *irrational violence* of Palestinians are familiar. Their tone recalls for me the kind of language used in the documentary we watched in Sunday School about the Israelis and their Arab neighbors. Post 9/11 sentiments intensified these discourses. CFOIC is single-minded in its appeal to American Christians to provide direct support not to Israel broadly, but directly to Israeli settlements in the West Bank, and it regularly and explicitly uses Biblical and theological references and ideas to make these appeals.

What I Believe About Christian Zionist Theology

I am focused on how these Christian Zionist claims function in relationship to Israeli settlement initiatives in Palestine. At this moment, I find myself generally alienated from Zionist pockets of evangelical theology, even dismissive of them. But how do I receive and evaluate the Biblical acceptability of Zionist theological claims? To clarify my personal position on these questions, I reread Biblical texts that I have read many times throughout my life and reflected on my current beliefs and perspectives, without taking the time to build a whole case for them.

As a Christian, I take the Bible to be God's words. I accept the Biblical narratives about Abraham and Sarah as historical accounts. God specially communicated with them, calling them to leave their homeland and promising to make Abraham the father of a new nation. God fulfilled this covenant with the deliverance of the Hebrews from Egypt, the giving of the law at Sinai, the passing through the Jordan river, and the conquest of the land of Canaan. Due to idolatry and injustice, Israel was violently expelled from the land into exile in Babylon. Old Testament prophecies such as those in the books of Isaiah and Daniel anticipate the rebuilding of the temple following the exile, and, Christologically, the coming of Jesus. These prophecies were largely fulfilled with the rebuilding of Jerusalem, events described by Ezra and Nehemiah (Burge, 2014; Isaac, 2015). Thus, I reject the modern reinterpretation of these prophecies to refer to contemporary developments in the Middle East. The New Testament Gospels—Matthew, Mark, Luke, and John—recount the life of Jesus. Together with other New Testament books, they introduce a new covenant that fulfills and extends the promises God made to Abraham (Burge, 2010; Katanacho, 2013; Wright, 1994). In Christ, all nations can be part of the people of God and receive God's promises for spiritual life and salvation. The book of Revelation is written in an apocalyptic genre, not historical; thus, it is intended to create a strong theological impression. The historical events that are anticipated in Revelation occurred in the first century with the Roman destruction of the Temple in Jerusalem, but the book also presents a theological vision of the redemptive role of Jesus, depicted as a slain lamb, and his people in the context of a world of evil and warring nations. Those who would follow Jesus from all nations are thus called to selflessly love the whole world as God does until He brings history to a close.

Reading these prophetic and apocalyptic passages as largely fulfilled in past events had obvious implications for Christian Zionism. The creation of the state of Israel in 1948 was not a theological event per se. It is better understood as a modern, secular, sociopolitical development that has been theologized post facto to carry divine meaning. The Israeli occupation of the West Bank and Gaza in 1967 is also eschatologically insignificant. It is better explained as an expansionistic, militarized, competitive, neoliberal, and settler-colonial phenomenon which is, likewise, theologized retroactively. Thus, there are not two distinct peoples of God, as Christian Zionism suggests. There is one people of God, comprised of all Jews and Gentiles who have been redeemed through Jesus. Until the Christological fulfillment, God was uniquely present in the Temple in Jerusalem, where believers could go to offer sacrifices and worship. In Christ, the people of God, from all nations, have become God's embodied dwelling place. Thus, although the land of Israel contains important religious significance historically, the modern state of Israel is not *theologically exceptional*. I am not commenting on whether Israel's modern political existence is legitimate, but whether its existence is Biblically warranted or rooted.

In line with core Christian Zionist doctrine, the so-called New Christian Zionism (McDermott, 2016) also claimed, "The return of Jews from all over the world to their land […] is part of the fulfillment of biblical prophecy" (p. 12), and the "people of Israel continue to be significant for the history of redemption, and that the land of Israel, which is at the heart of the covenantal promises, continues to be important to God's providential purposes" (p. 13). As I have explained these are claims I have come to believe are not biblically necessary nor, more to the point, biblically correct. Theologically, one of the main innovations these scholars claim for the New Christian Zionism is its separation from dispensational theological paradigms; yet, by their own acknowledgement, there are historical streams of Christian Zionism that pre-date dispensationalism, so the claim of innovation may not be exactly correct. The editor poses the question (McDermott, 2016, p. 11), what is the New Christian Zionism, but then does not answer the question directly, instead suggesting the rest of the book will provide the answer. The editor takes the balance of the introduction to explain what it is *not*—they claim it is not dispensationalism, not merely nationalism, not merely Christian, not land theft, not racism, and not theocracy. It appears the work might not be as theologically innovative as it is an emerging theological-political synthesis that seeks to reframe Christian Zionism in terms that are more broadly appealing to contemporary audiences across denominations and religious communities.

Christian Zionism and Settler Colonialism

Hummel (2009) helpfully noted, "The recency of organized Christian Zionism suggests that it is not an obvious consequence of evangelical theology, nor is cooperation between evangelicals and Jews a natural political arrangement" (p. 2). This leaves historically particular reasons for the alliance. Counter to the notion that American and British evangelicals developed Christian Zionism as an organic outgrowth of their larger theological commitments, in the following section I argue that evangelical Zionist theology parallels and supports settler colonial tropes resulting in theology that supplies theological endorsement for settler colonialism. This section draws on Veracini's (2010) forms of settler colonial transfer (see previous discussion) to demonstrate the embeddedness of these ideas in Christian Zionism.

Settler Colonialism and Israel

Building on Wolfe (2006), Veracini (2010) conceptualized a particular type of colonialism characterized by replacement of an Indigenous civilian population with a colonial civilian population, what Veracini termed *transfer* (p. 34). Thus, in contrast to colonialism in general, in which the metropole dominates a new territory for the purpose of extracting economic value, settler colonialism is about expropriating the land itself and pushing out current inhabitants. Veracini theorized that settlers, in pursuing the moral authority to enact these transfers, seek to maximize their status along two spectra: indigeneity and righteousness. Thus, settler groups seek to increase their claim to being Indigenous while undermining the credibility of rival claims. Settlers also seek to increase their status as virtuous, innocent, noble, and moral, while increasing rivals' status as degraded, uncivilized, untrustworthy, or savage. Put differently, settler colonial groups rationalize expropriation based on being Indigenous and deserving.

Although Veracini (2010) might not put it in these terms, this settler colonial project seems to operate in relative terms: A settlement community does not have to prove absolute indigeneity, merely that they have a greater quantity or quality of indigeneity than any other claimant group. Likewise, such a community does not have to prove absolute indigeneity, but only more indigeneity than any other group. By Veracini's theory, Israelis living in settlements in the West Bank, seek to compete with

Palestinians as more truly Indigenous and more truly pure and deserving. Much of the settler rhetoric about ancient claims to the land rooted in the Old Testament seems to confirm Veracini's insights in the Israel/Palestine context.

Settler colonialism ignites and sustains ideological and demographic warfare, not to mention armed conflict, between colonial settler entity and Indigenous community. In this multidimensional physical and conceptual space, transfer of communities and land is executed. Tactics of transfer, again from Veracini (2010), include necropolitical transfer (ethnic cleansing), deportation, conceptual displacement (in which Palestinians are reframed more generically as Arabs, thus deprived of their specific Indigenous claim to Palestine), perception transfer (the presence of Indigenous communities are left out of the frame of reference; as in the historical narrative that Jewish immigrants settled an unoccupied desert), administrative transfer (redrawing administrative and municipal boundaries and the rights attendant with citizenship in these zones), settler indigenization (in which settlers are reframed as Indigenous), and narrative transfer (where the Indigenous society is reframed as hopelessly backward or immorally brutal). For Veracini, Israeli colonial groups wield these tactics to replace Palestinians as the most Indigenous and deserving claimant group in the conflict over the land. The following analysis focuses on settler indigenization, conceptual displacement, perception transfer, and narrative transfer.

Settler Indigenization

One of the central claims of Christian Zionism is that the Jewish people belong in historic Palestine, that they have a legitimate claim of Indigenous connection to that land. Indeed, Christian Zionism theologizes this claim by arguing that God has given the land once and forever to the Jewish people as their homeland. In retrospect, there are several periods toward which this Christian Zionist assertion to Jewish indigeneity has been deployed, if not historically, then in retrospect: these include the end of the nineteenth century and first half of the twentieth century, during Jewish migrations to Palestine (Aliyah) and since the 1967 war, as Israeli settlers built settlements in the West Bank (and in Gaza until the disengagement in 2005). Contemporary Christian Zionist material speaks to both periods.

In his speech at the ceremonial opening of the U.S. embassy in Jerusalem, evangelical pastor John Hagee (2018), a Christian Zionist leader, gave the benediction: "It was you, oh Lord, who gathered the exiles and brought them home again." The land is cast as an eternal *home*land. He continued, "Jerusalem is and always shall be the eternal capital of the Jewish people." Sometimes the claim that the Jewish people are Indigenous to historic Palestine is the thesis of persuasive discourses and not merely assumed or nakedly asserted. In his introduction to *The New Christian Zionism: Fresh Perspectives on Israel & the Land*, McDermott (2016) took several pages to demonstrate that "[…] Jews have lived in the land of Israel for three thousand years, all the while thinking of themselves as Jews in the homeland for Jewish culture" (pp. 16–18). Countless other examples could be offered as the claim that Jews are the rightful, Indigenous inhabitants of the land is perhaps the most definitive claim of Christian Zionism. This Christian Zionist claim to Israeli indigeneity extends Veracini's (2010) settler indigenization concept into the realm of Christian theology.

Conceptual Displacement

Veracini (2010) defined conceptual displacement as reframing an Indigenous group with a more generic, superordinate identity, thus depriving them of specific claims to specific land. In the context of Israel/Palestine, this is common, as Palestinians are regularly referenced throughout Zionist literature by the more generic ethnic moniker of Arabs. Reframing Palestinian identity in this way destabilizes Palestinians' claim to historic Palestine while implying these Arabs have a much larger homeland to which they belong.

Responding to criticisms about the theft of land in Palestine during the 1948 war—Palestinians refer to it as the *Nakba* (the catastrophe)—McDermott (2016) uses the less precise *Arab* or *Arabs* 17 times in reference to the more than 750,000 Palestinians who lost their land in Palestine at that time. McDermott's word choice is illustrative: "It is true that hundreds of thousands of Arabs felt compelled to abandon their homes during the 1948 Arab-Israel War. They fled the violence of war, which was begun by the Arab nations, not Israel" (p. 22). If the people who felt compelled to flee their homes were Arabs, and the nations to which they fled were Arab, then the logic of the argument suggests they are not refugees after all and have no claim to Palestine. Dennis Prager, a conservative Jewish commentator in the United States with a sizable evangelical following, produced a film for his online platform in which he articulated: "There are twenty-two Arab states in the world, stretching from the Atlantic Ocean to the Indian Ocean. There is one Jewish state in the world, and it is about the size of New Jersey" (Prager, n.d.). Again, framing Palestinian refugees broadly as Arabs, disconnects them from the geography of their homeland in Palestine and paves the way for arguments such as the ones McDermott and Prager have made.

Perception Transfer

For Veracini (2010), perception transfer is the process by which Indigenous groups are rendered invisible or by which the frame of reference excludes them. This can happen through the revision of collective memory that removes the Indigenous experience from the realm of historical understanding. It might happen through the dehumanization of Indigenous people who are otherwise physically present and yet removed from the frame of civilized society.

Perception transfer is a ubiquitous expression of Israeli settler colonialism in Palestine. The mythology that Jewish immigrants arrived in an empty land and *made the desert bloom* expresses this idea. Another example is the expression *a land without a people for a people without a land* popularized by Christian restorationists in the nineteenth century, arguing that Jews suffering under the pogroms in Eastern Europe should be allowed to immigrate to Palestine. Either scenario reflects the settler colonial tactic of perception transfer. In "the deal of the century," plan for Israel proposed by the Trump administration (White House, 2020)—a plan deeply influenced by Trump's Christian Zionist allies—the maps include the names of Israeli cities while excluding the names of Palestinian cities. When Christian Zionist narratives about the land exclude attention to Palestinians, they resonate with settler colonial efforts at perception transfer.

Passages Israel, which I discussed in an earlier section, is a nonprofit that "offers Christian college students with leadership potential a fresh and innovative approach to experiencing the Holy Land" (Passages website). Although Passages Israel does not officially claim a Christian Zionist position, it uses Christian Zionist tropes and ideology. The map Passages gives to student travelers used a subtle line to mark the boundary between Israel and the West Bank (it is hard to find), but used a bright, bold line to circumscribe one large territory that includes the state of Israel, the West Bank, Gaza, and the Golan Heights, as if, to the uninitiated, this whole area was the state of Israel. The map advances a settler colonial transfer of perception.

Narrative Transfer

Veracini (2010) described narrative transfer as the process by which Indigenous society is characterized as hopelessly backward, thus unable to survive or thrive in modern, global, technological society. Discursively, the implication is that any struggle for survival stems not from oppression, but from an intrinsic unsuitability for contemporary pressures. Although Veracini did not expand in this direction, narrative transfer could be situated in a larger taxonomy of tactics that seek to characterize Indigenous cultures as unfit for participation in modern civilized society. This process is perhaps nowhere more clearly expressed than in the discourse that Palestinians are constitutionally tribalistic and violent (Asad, 2007). Prager (n.d.) again: "If tomorrow Israel laid down its arms and announced we will fight no more, what would happen? […] There would be an immediate destruction of the State of Israeli and mass murder of its Jewish population." Such characterizations function discursively to position Israel on the moral high ground and to frame Palestinians and other Arab neighbors as undeserving of normal rights to self-determination.

At the same ceremony marking the opening of the U.S. embassy, Hagee (2018) proclaimed "Let every Islamic terrorist hear this message: that Israel lives." This occasion, being what it was, held clear implications for Palestinians, who claim Eastern Jerusalem as their future capital. Thus, the reference should almost certainly be read as a characterization of Palestinians—who would dispute the Israeli expropriation of Eastern Jerusalem—to be terrorists. This is the only reference Hagee made to Palestine or Palestinians in the benediction. Such characterizations blur the morally important difference between a society that contains terrorists and one that is terroristic. These characterizations also redirect critical scrutiny away from the considerable violence and oppression of the Israeli state against the Palestinians, and from the legitimate moral claims Palestinians have against colonial impingement (Asad, 2007).

Discursive tactics active in rationalizing settlement activities in the West Bank may or may not directly shape Christian Zionist constructs, but these constructs certainly resonate, complement, and even adopt the settler colonial tactics discussed herein. Ideas such as the emptiness of Palestine before Jewish immigration, the endemic brutality of Arabs, and other settler colonial tropes find parallel, theologized constructions in certain expressions of Christian Zionism. Such an ideological relationship, between an active settler colonial project and a subset of the Christian theological community, carries with it a range of concrete implications in practice and policy.

Discussion

Referring to Israel and the United States, Kaplan (2018) noted, "Cultural perceptions, to be sure, do not dictate policies. They do, however, create a perceptual field in interaction with those policies and political ideas from which a consensus emerges" (p. 3). I have argued that Christian Zionism functions as a theological construct that parallels and aids the Israeli settler colonial project in Palestine. As such, it is akin to

Kaplan's "perceptual field" that interacts with and mediates policy formation and maintenance. For my purposes, I understand policy loosely as definitions, expectations, and prescriptions encoded in organizational and institutional documents and understandings.

I briefly explore three areas of intersection between the Christian Zionist "perceptual field" and areas of policy and practice. First, Christian Zionism forms a discursive ground for a key constituency that supports national, pro-Israel policy. Second, Christian Zionism influences pro-Israel ecclesial policies and practices among denominations and churches. Third, Christian Zionism and associated political commitments and perceptions impact Christian higher education policy and practice. Each of these areas is provisional and requires further study to refine and ground the argument.

Having received $142.3B overall in fiscal and material aid since its founding, Israel is the number one recipient of U.S. foreign assistance in the world (Sharp, 2019, p. 2). This figure should come as no surprise, as the United States is known around the world as an unqualified friend and ally of the state of Israel. Further, a large portion of the assistance has been earmarked for missile defense and other military development. Israel is the first nation outside of the United States to purchase and operate F-35s from the United States, considered to be the most technologically advanced fighter jets in the world (Sharp, 2019). Israel is also the beneficiary of U.S. diplomatic support in the United Nations and direct international relationships. Behind this diplomatic history and current practice, the political establishment relies on a variety of constituencies for support, evangelicals, and other Christian Zionists among them. Donald Trump's administration was a case in point. President Trump's support from conservative evangelicals, many of whom are Christian Zionists, is broadly known. Thus, the pro-Israeli bias of Trump's "Deal of a Century" should not be surprising. Already mentioned, the ceremony at the opening of the U.S. embassy in Jerusalem is another clear case of the intersection of Christian Zionist beliefs with U.S. foreign policy in Israel/Palestine.

Conservative Protestants in the United States tend to identify Israel as uniquely enlightened, democratic, and righteous in the context of its larger region. Although they are likely to perceive Palestine and Palestinians as terroristic in nature (Asad, 2007), they also advance other discourses as well. For example, conservative Protestants, who tend to think about the religious persecution of Christians around the world, may identify with Palestinian Christians whom they perceive to be persecuted by the Muslim majority in Palestine. Such a narrative can function as a rhetorical device to accomplish discursive aims that align with the terrorist narrative—that Palestinians are culturally inclined toward violence and oppression. What are the implications of such beliefs? As far as church practice is concerned, such components may affect giving patterns, where revenue from Christian charity is directed. It also affects the substantial religious tourism industry of the U.S. church. As denominations, churches, and para-church organizations engage in such tourism, these beliefs influence trip itineraries and impact who received the economic benefits of the industry. The impact of tourism is discussed further.

Conservative Christian higher education is also a site for the intersection of Christian Zionist beliefs and concrete policy implications. The Council for Christian Colleges and Universities is a membership association engaging 150 Christian colleges in the United States whose missions are "Christ-centered and rooted in the historic Christian faith" (CCCU website). The CCCU hosted a massive bronze statue depicting the Lion of Judah, a symbol of Israel, at their 2018 International Forum (Figure 9). The statue went on to tour the country, stopping briefly at the National Religious Broadcasters national conference and then was donated to the state of Israel (Greiner, 2018). It now stands in Bloomfield Park, overlooking the Old City of Jerusalem. Passages Israel articulated their rationale for engaging Christian college students—these students will go on to "pastor churches, lead ministries and businesses, develop foreign policy, run for office" (Passages website) and more. Passages brings hundreds of Christian college students and their professors to Israel each year. A quick review of their itineraries reveals an overtly one-sided perspective aligned with a Christian Zionist approach (Passages guidebook).

Figure 9

Bronze Lion of Judah Statue on Display at the Council of Christian Colleges and Universities International Forum in 2018

Kaplan (2018) concluded her study of U.S./Israeli relations with an encouragement to look "beyond romantic reflections of the past—promised lands, chosen peoples, frontier pioneers, wars of independence." Doing so "would enable us to see the darker shadows of shared exceptionalism: the fusion of moral value with military force, the defiance of international law, the rejection of refugees and immigrants in countries that were once known as havens" (p. 280). This is where I situate my conclusion as well. Regardless of the motives with which Christian Zionism is held, the belief system provides a certain level of theological cover for the Israeli settler colonial enterprise in the West Bank and Gaza. Adopting an understanding that knowledge is socially constructed and generated by those with power could allow for a more nuanced and inclusive approach to Palestine and Palestinians among conservative American Protestants.

CHAPTER 3

SPATIAL MACHINERY: SETTLER COLONIAL CONFIGURATIONS AND EPISTEMOLOGICAL IMPLICATIONS

The notion that your *zip code is your destiny* is particularly poignant in Palestine. The current form of occupation and settler colonialism in the West Bank is advanced through the control of populations through the control of space: huge concrete wall akin to the Berlin wall, checkpoints, zones where Palestinians are permitted, zones where they are not permitted, and control over where Palestinians can construct buildings (Figure 10). These are all spatial mechanisms.

The spatial control that is such a pronounced part of life in Bethlehem carries implications for administrators, teachers, and students in higher education. The president of one of the colleges in Bethlehem lives in Israel and commutes through a checkpoint each day. Some students enrolled at institutions in Bethlehem wake up each morning in refugee camps. Faculty who used to teach in Bethlehem cannot anymore because driving the long way around the system of walls and check points is now too long of a commute. Some students have missed classes because they are held under house arrest or detention without charge. Some students have had to drop out because their family home was demolished, and their family had to move away. Some students at universities in Bethlehem have never been outside of Bethlehem.

The wall has been written about in a political frame of reference. The stories about the origin of the possibility of the wall, the deliberations that led to the route of the wall, and the discourses that interpret the wall are political stories. But the wall is many other things as well. Among them, the wall is *pedagogical* (not necessarily in the positive

Figure 10

Settlements, Seam Zone, and the Wall Relative to Bethlehem. Map Created by the Author

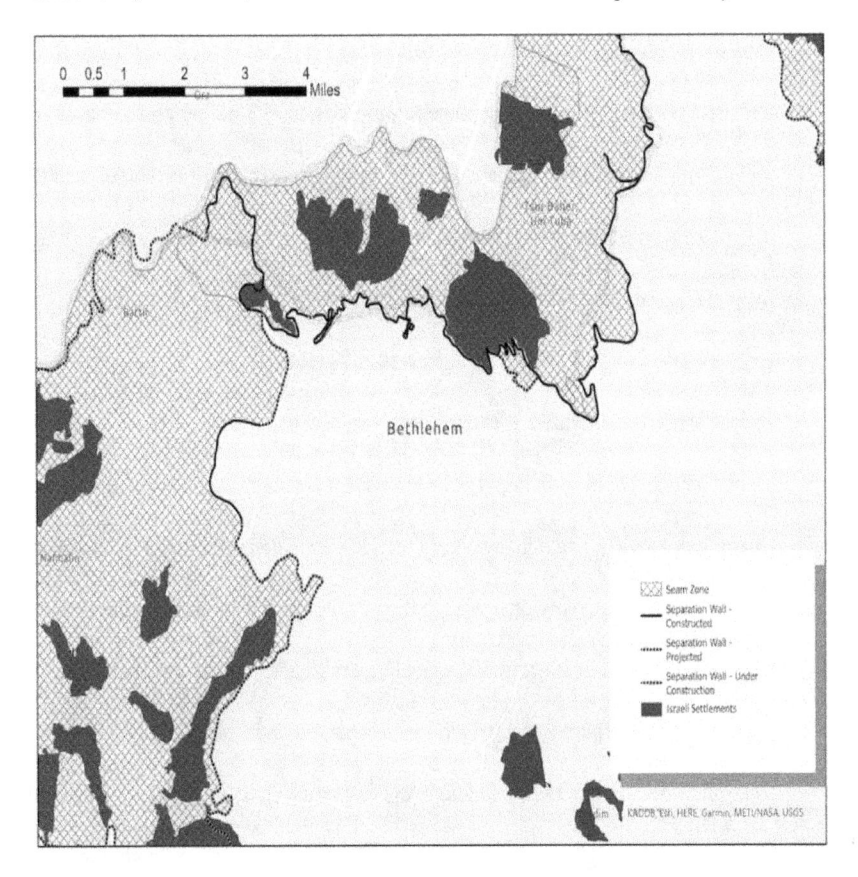

sense, but in the more modest sense that it impacts knowledge). It makes certain kinds of learning more difficult or impossible and creates conditions for alternative forms of "knowledge" to gain the advantage.

What are the physical features of the settler colonial space in which Palestinian educators and students pursue their work and how are these features experienced? There are different ways space is produced (spatialization), whereby absolute (natural) space is transformed into more complex forms of space. The meanings of these more complex forms of space are interpreted socially (social space). Lefebvre (1992) argued that space is socially constructed. These constructions effect practices and understandings of space. This shift highlights the importance of attending not only to spaces and their meanings, but also to their prior origins and means of production. For our purposes, that suggests the importance not only of exploring educational spaces, occupation spaces, and the meanings people see in them, but also to the settler colonial struggle to define spaces and the place Palestinian higher education may play in these struggles.

Literature Review

Space is configured. It is put together to perform functions. Walls are erected to shelter families, hold earth in place, keep prisoners in, keep enemies out, direct crowds where they should go, and many other functions. This functional nature of space exists at many scales from an individual who configures their workspace to multinational, even multi-continental infrastructures like pipelines, railroads, and mining operations. Indeed, there are not a few purposes to which space is put, but a dizzying multiplicity of layered configurations and functions. Although this vast multiplicity of configurations might look like chaos from a certain vantage, certain bundles of configurations might function a little like an operating system in the sense that there are central logics and complementary functions.

Spatial configurations usually have official or declared functions. Yet, spatial configurations also have undeclared functions (Easterling, 2014). In the Palestinian West Bank, the declared function of the Israeli-built separation barrier is security for the State of Israel, yet it also functions to sever Palestinian land in the West Bank from Palestinian populations. What is a road for? A road enables the flow of traffic along its course. And yet, it also performs other functions. It not only enhances flow *along* its course, but simultaneously retards flow *across* its path. The road not only connects points along its path with each other—but it also divides the world into which it is laid in half and can be, in a very real sense, a barrier. Planners approach this retardation of flow from the space on one side to space on the other side as a merely logistical problem to be overcome by the introduction of a bridge or an intersection, but, in other situations, the blocking function of a road might be welcomed and leveraged strategically. The declared and undeclared functions of spatial configurations in Palestine create a unique and challenging landscape in which to produce and transfer knowledge. Palestinians living in the West Bank exist in space that has been highly configured by others. This study draws on three theoretical approaches to understanding a nature of spatial configuration in the West Bank and its functions: spatial production (de Certeau, 2011; Lefebvre, 1992), settler colonial transfer (Masalha, 1992; Veracini, 2010), and infrastructure space (Easterling, 2014).

Spatial Production

Space and land are contested and controlled in the Palestinian West Bank. Indeed, settler colonial contexts anywhere highlight the stakes involved in spatial domination. But in everyday life in many parts of the world, space tends to fade to the background. It is a void, a container in which bodies and objects reside and inter-relate—as a backdrop to other objects of focus, it is often taken for granted. Unfortunately, although space can be taken for granted, its influence is active and dynamic. In this study, I want to think explicitly about space as not merely a void but as a subject that acts on prospects for knowledge production in Palestine.

Space is socially constructed. Space yields to social interventions. The Roosevelt Road underpass near my house that runs beneath Highway 355 west of Chicago was produced by social processes at a given time in the past, and yet it exists today, in this world, as a feature that shapes the space in its locale, prospects for movement, and access to the freeway. Thus, today's space is socially produced by the past and present activity of groups. It is not only the physical aspects of space, but also the symbolic and conceptual dimensions. The divisions, zones, labels, meanings, and regulations that are part of understanding and navigation of space are also socially constructed through legal, cultural, even religious processes. The speed limit on highway 90 is produced by groups; the signage that communicates regulations and labels places, the names given to roads, cities, and states, are also produced.

Space is always changing. Picking up this idea, Massey (2005) noted the ever-changing, always transforming nature of space. This insight that space is constantly changing resonates with Lefevre's (1992) point that space and time must be considered together, that space cannot be properly conceived of synchronically (as a snapshot) but rather diachronically (space over the course of time). Yet, the plasticity of space is not equally available to all populations. De Certeau (2011) noted the role of elites in constructing the urban environment. Interventions can transform the character of space in fleeting or long-term ways. Bridges, buildings, walls, roads, signs, monuments, mines, canals, and other spatial features may endure, shaping prospects for human action in space for generations or even millennia.

De Certeau (2011) posited two categories of people: social elites, who produce the basic structures of the social and physical world; and everyday people, who consume that which has been created, moving in physical environments, and receiving goods and services offered. De Certeau's idea of strategies and tactics corresponds to these groups: Elites' productions of the world are strategies and create the structures within which everyday life occurs and the activities of everyday people in these structures are tactics. De Certeau utilized the image of New York as a metaphor to describe the production of strategies by elites (the built environment of skyscrapers, streets, traffic lights, and other infrastructural dimensions) and tactics (the ways people move through the city, sometimes behaving in predicted ways, but other times transgressing expectations using short cuts or detours. De Certeau's strategies and tactics are comparable in some ways to the situation in the West Bank. Occupation infrastructure is constructed with implicit, sometimes explicit, projections for how they will produce behaviors from those whose lives are contained or transected by these infrastructures. But De Certeau recognized such strategies are not absolute in their power over the behavior of their social objects. According to de Certeau, there are no absolute objects, but people always have at least some degree of freedom to improvise as they respond to the presence of a new wall, a new rule, a new prohibition, or a new entity.

Knowledge about space is discursive in nature—groups with power can advance their own "truth" about a space/place. Such knowledge advances the interests of the groups that utilize them. When a group has power not only to advance its own discourses about a place, but also to reshape the place itself, the place assumes a discursive nature as well. The place contains spatial arguments, topographies and infrastructures that *make arguments*. An example of this can be seen driving through Pacific Northwest on roads with a visual buffer of woods hugging the sides of the road, when the rest of the mountain has been clear cut. In these situations, where a group has power to reshape topography, the resulting spatial transformations do not only "make arguments," but they also transform knowledge prospects for those who live there. In the West Bank, for example, Palestinians have differential prospects for knowledge of the land than from other Palestinians outside of the West Bank and from Israelis. For those living in environments that have been reshaped by powerful others, their agency is not eradicated, but it does encounter new impositions. The process of countering the spatial arguments embedded by others in their environment is also discursive but happens from within this transformed topography. The risks involved in making such arguments, in advancing such knowledge (counter arguments), are greater for those living in these environments than for those whose discourses and transformations are initiated from elsewhere. Israeli-built infrastructure in Palestine can also be read as a spatial discourse, as a text that argues that the West Bank is Israel.

Because interests differ across spaces, spaces emerge differently, resulting in different spatial configurations. Such differential configurations are like incompatible computer systems, operating with hardware and software that may contain different levels of interoperability and incompatibility. In other words, spaces can be structured by logics that are incomprehensible to each other. Space is influential of human behavior and life patterns. Spatial configurations create or reinforce patterns of behavior. The velvet handrails do not only keep people in line; they also show where to queue up. The road not only conveys traffic; it also shows where to drive. The gate doesn't only open, it shows where to cross. Neither fully deterministic nor fully yielding, space deeply shapes human action and is shaped by it.

Knowledge and practice are linked to the material world and its spaces. Not only is knowledge processed in spaces, but also in ubiquitous and inevitable fashion, knowledge and practice are constructed in dialogue with spaces. De Certeau (2011) suggested logics of strategy—imposed from above by political or economic elites, upon the built environment—and of tactics, with which people respond as they improvise from inside these environments. They never act like robots—they do not respond to these environments as intended from above—but always in dialogue with the environments that contain them. Space and material configurations that organize space also advance or deny equity and access for various groups who make their lives within them (Soja, 2010), so spatial configurations are not only meaningful as epistemological environments, but also moral and ethical ones.

In these transformed, discursive environments, epistemic production takes on salience to those imposed upon. Social and institutional structures that produce such knowledge are presented with new questions about the role they will play. Their activities may be a complex interplay between cooperation, resistance, survival, etc. Institutions of higher learning in Palestine are presented with such a prospect and do respond in complex ways. As member organizations of the Palestinian Authority (PA), some of the criticisms of the PA as structurally beholden to Israeli authority can be extended to them. But in other places and spaces in these institutions, knowledge about Palestinian space is advanced against alternatives.

Settler Colonial Transfer

One of the seminal articles on settler colonialism appeared in a journal dedicated to scholarship about genocide (Wolfe, 2006) and advanced the theme of elimination of

Native populations as a distinctive feature of settler colonialism. But it is not always clear that Palestine as a people is being *eliminated* as much as it is being dominated, exploited, fractured, and dispossessed of its land slowly through settler colonial opportunism. Settler colonial studies describes the notion of *transfer* (Veracini, 2010; Wolfe, 2006), which denotes a wide range of processes to displace Indigenous populations to clear space for settlement. Settler colonialism can be thought of as domination for the purpose of transfer (Veracini, 2010). In the U.S./North American context, warfare, destruction of the environment, and treaties have played roles in the transfer of Native Americans away from ancestral land and its settlement by European Americans, but the combination of processes can differ across cases. Settler colonialism has been applied to the Palestinian context many times (e.g., Khalidi, 2020), and transfer, most specifically, has been as well (e.g., Masalha, 1992).

Transfer does not absolutely have to mean the physical removal of people—it can also refer to the social or legal displacement of a population in ways that allow for the acquisition of their land, which may lead to circumstances akin to apartheid. Nor does transfer have to be immediate or suddenly catastrophic—it can involve the construction of a set of uncomfortable or unfavorable circumstances that lead to the slow dwindling of a population or to the semi-voluntary emigration of younger generations. In Veracini's (2010) catalogue of tactics, transfer can also be enacted through assimilation and "uplift." Native American boarding schools, for example, could position themselves in a civilizing and humanitarian frame, yet participate in cultural transfer of Native American space and populations (Adams, 2020).

Veracini (2010) catalogued dozens of disparate tactics that have been employed across contexts to enact transfer. Many of these tactics are discernible in Israel/Palestine, whether in the past or currently practiced. The Nakba certainly involved the raw use of force (transfer through *military liquidation*) to displace more that 700,000 Palestinians from their homes in areas that became the state of Israel. Palestinians are mass incarcerated (transfer through *incarceration*). Palestinian land is appropriated by Israeli settlement organizations (transfer through *transfer of settlers*).

Many tactics on Veracini's (2010) list are more discursive and epistemological than physically violent. The use of more superordinate categories to label Palestinians as Arabs seeks to loosen the distinctive claim Palestinians make to Palestinian space (transfer through *conceptual displacement*). Israeli settlers claim Indigenous status (transfer through *settler indigenization*). Palestinian society is framed as hopelessly backward and in need of the sponsorship of a more developed country (transfer through *narrative*). Indeed, landscapes have both a material dimension (i.e., what can be observed with the eye) and a textual dimension (i.e., the symbolic and interpretive vision that appears in people's minds; Fields, 2017). Both dimensions become contested battlegrounds in Native struggles against settler colonial power. These formulations resonate with Said's (1978) notion of imaginative geography, the processes of reimagining the meaning of a landscape to justify its appropriation (e.g., as I write, Putin is invading Ukraine, and advancing wartime rhetoric that Ukraine is home to ethnic Russians that need to be liberated, an example of imaginative geography).

Tactics of transfer are rarely used in isolation but combined into complex structures of transfer. For example, the combined use of maps to present a settler vision of land, of legal institutions to create legitimated paths for acquisition of land, and of landscape architecture to transform the land is a repeated pattern across multiple settler colonial cases (Fields, 2017). Thus, the "law and the fence play complementary roles as instruments of force" (Fields, 2017, p. xiii). Because multiple of these tactics of transfer are discernable in this study's geographical case (Bethlehem), this study advances with *transfer*, rather than *elimination*, as a main analytical framework.

Infrastructurespace

This study focuses on the ways infrastructure is used to advance and consolidate transfer in the West Bank. To think about infrastructure, I rely heavily on Easterling's (2014) theoretical account of *infrastructure space*, a concept that highlights the politics and power dynamics of infrastructure. Infrastructure space

> behaves like spatial software. And while we also do not typically think of static objects and volumes in urban space as having agency, infrastructure space is doing something. Like an operating system, the medium of infrastructure space makes certain things possible and other things impossible. (Easterling, 2014, p. 14)

Fresh water pipes, roads, barriers, checkpoints, electricity, cell towers, and internet cables are all examples of what Easterling calls *object forms.* Object forms all have various functions, to carry water, to provide access by automobile to different locations, and to distribute electricity for example. But at another level, these object forms of infrastructure, embody what Easterling termed *active forms. Active forms,* in contrast, are discernable functions that may go unstated but constitute an infrastructural *disposition.*

Consider a few active forms include *multipliers*, *switches*, and *topologies*. Some technologies create new conditions that effect objects across a whole field. These active forms are *multipliers*. Easterling (2014) suggested the introduction of the car as a multiplier, as it created conditions for builders to include attached garages in residential home designs, a feature that is now nearly ubiquitous in some locales. Other technologies and infrastructures can control conditions at a distance. These are *switches* or *remotes*. A gate controls access to the other side of the fence. By locking or unlocking the gate, conditions beyond the gate can be controlled. Other examples include freeway interchanges, dams, and checkpoints. Assemblages of multipliers, switches, and other active forms can create *wiring topologies:* "Just as an electronic network is wired to support specific activities, so can space be 'wired' to encourage some activities and routines over others" (Easterling, 2014, p. 78). Assemblages of infrastructure can have *dispositions* to certain effects, which are activated when certain conditions are fulfilled, like a ball, whose disposition is to roll down the hill when it is nudged to the edge. The gap between the explicit or official function of an assemblage and its disposition is a *discrepancy*. Easterling said, "The misalignment between the activity of an organization and its stated intent is often the first signal of an undeclared disposition" (p. 88).

Research Question

There are countless works about the ways space is controlled in the Palestinian West Bank (e.g., Peteet, 2017; Sfard, 2018; Weizman, 2007). These analyses provide clearer understanding of the general social and political implications of the separation barrier, the checkpoints, the settlements, the bypass roads, and more. This study seeks to engage this literature and ask additional questions about the physical relationships between these infrastructures and higher educational spaces in Bethlehem. Likewise, settler colonial theory is well-expounded elsewhere—this study takes transfer as a starting point and basis for an exploration of the ways transfer is enacted in physical and discursive space around higher educational space in Bethlehem. Thus, the research question for this study is *how do nearby spatial configurations of occupation and transfer influence prospects for Palestinian knowledge production in general and education more specifically?* This is a question about the epistemological implications of the settler colonial displacements for Palestinians. What do infrastructures of displacement and control over bodies, places, and mobility mean for knowledge production? Where does infrastructure restrict or inhibit the access and presence that leads to new knowledge? Where does infrastructure of occupation and transfer impinge into educational space? Where do infrastructures that control mobility lay across the paths needed for education to proceed?

Method

This study is a theoretical exploration of the pedagogical role that space plays, one could say its *knowledge effects*. Attention is given most precisely to the politico-military control of space and the pressures it creates to produce educational spaces. The exploration concludes with a series of questions about roles higher education might play in the epistemological spaces constituted by settler colonial policies of transfer. As an empirical basis for this exploration, I conducted a mapping study to overlay population and infrastructures in and around Bethlehem, Palestine in a series of GIS maps.

Research Design

This study is part of a larger regional case study on higher education in Bethlehem, Palestine. Case study as a method allows for the inclusion of a range of types of data, such as interviews, archived materials, databases, and documents (Yin, 2017). The larger study seeks to understand the settler colonial pressures within which the Palestinian higher education system operates and its structural and pedagogical initiatives, particularly in Bethlehem. In the course of this larger study, particularly in the interviews with Palestinian educators and students, questions about the role of spatial control and its roles in collective knowledge production surfaced repeatedly. The present study seeks to explore these questions. Situating maps at the center of this more focused study allowed space to come to the fore as a primary focus, as a context in which knowledge production is constrained and activated. For example, multiple faculty and administrators told stories about students from East Jerusalem who must come through Checkpoint 300 any time they need to be on campus for classes, meetings, or time in the library or the studio. These stories raised spatial questions about the routes and obstacles experienced specifically by students from a certain spatial area and the unique constraints they face as they seek new learning and knowledge production. Other stories emerged about youth who increasingly perceive previously familiar spaces and cities as more foreign. These stories were often connected to observations about the demobilization of Palestinians within the West Bank due to checkpoints, Israeli settlements, restricted roads, and other mechanisms.

Case study also allows research interests to be somewhat flexible and contingent, based on emerging data. This naturalistic approach (Lincoln & Guba, 1985) in the larger case study led, in this case, to this more specific sub-study on space as these themes emerged in the interviews. Another important consideration in this research design is the difference between synchronic and diachronic perspectives on space (Lefebvre, 1992). Synchronic perspective is a way of considering space at a given instant. Diachronic perspective allows a research aperture to view the dynamics of space over time. This study combines both to some extent—the maps capture spatial configurations at a given moment in 2022, when they were generated, but the narrative elements from the interviews introduce a diachronic perspective that capture human experiences of these spaces over the course of multiple years.

Data Collection

I interviewed 25 Palestinian administrators and faculty at three institutions of higher learning in Bethlehem from August 2019 through March 2022. Given the travel lockdowns during the COVID-19 pandemic, I conducted most of these interviews online via Zoom video calls. I recorded these interviews and had the recordings transcribed verbatim. I uploaded these transcripts to a qualitative data analysis software (Dedoose) for closer reading and coding. The codes gave rise to higher order themes that are presented in another article. For purposes of this article, I draw on a limited set of relevant narratives to explore human experiences and perspectives on the physical environment near and around where higher education occurs in Bethlehem.

I used an ArcGIS base map and layers provided by the United Nations Office for the Coordination of Humanitarian Affairs (UNOCHA). OCHA uses these maps in their operations, but they are also often used by third party organizations as a basis for geographical, political, and natural resources research. By using GIS layers, I was able to analyze the relative position of Palestinian educational spaces, Israeli settlement spaces, and infrastructures of occupation and spatial control as well as routes and paths between these spaces or bypassing these spaces.

I also directly observed physical spaces in and around Bethlehem, once in June 2019 and again in March 2022. During these research trips, I observed the separation barrier at multiple points, toured refugee camps, toured three colleges and universities, passed through local checkpoints, observed students and faculty arriving to and navigating around campuses, and noticed the physical characteristics of campus spaces such as walls, gates, paths, signage, and architecture. I took pictures to document these spaces for later reference and analysis. I kept the geo location data function turned on to place the exact location of each picture. These locations are indicated on maps in the findings. I used color fields in some images presented in the findings to highlight spatial configurations and differentiate between Israeli and Palestinian used spaces.

Data Analysis

I conducted analysis within and across data types. Once relevant narratives were identified and selected from among the larger set of interviews, I read them closely and generated spatial themes based on observations or experiences that emerged in multiple interviews. For example, multiple participants talked about their experiences passing through Checkpoint 300. Multiple others described their experiences as a refugee in one of the refugee camps.

In working with the maps, after overlaying educational/campus locations with the locations of occupation- and settlement-related infrastructures and the locations of other key features such as refugee camps, I made a series of analytical observations. I noted where spaces overlap, where features are proximate, and where features are separated by distances. By connecting the interview narratives and direct observations with the physical representations in the maps, I was also able to identify human effects of physical infrastructure (Easterling's idea of *disposition*) and the disjunctions between the formal purpose of various infrastructures (usually security related) and the dispositions—these disjunctors are Easterling's (2014) idea of *discrepancy*.

Role of the Researcher

I like maps—I have for as long as I can remember. I like thinking about how space, geography, physical infrastructure, and human society layer, one over the other. I remember being fascinated when someone told me that the migration of ethnic groups flowed up the Appalachian valleys over time, and that distinctive accents and dialects are now nestled in neighboring mountain valleys as a result. Because of this interest of mine, I go out of my way to collect maps when I go to Palestine—the Israeli occupation of Palestine is, if nothing else, spatial, geographic, and physical, all dimensions that maps are well suited to depict.

There are two maps I've brought home that are particularly illuminating. The first is a political map I picked up at a Palestinian research center in Bethlehem. The areas under Palestinian jurisdiction are clearly marked in different colors, and the map includes physical infrastructure of the occupation such as the separation barrier, checkpoints, special jurisdictions, Israeli-only roads, and Israeli settlements. I received the second map from a Christian college student who had just returned from a trip to Israel with a Christian tour group from America and had received the map in a packet of other pro-Israel materials. This second map, which is labeled as a map of Israel, depicts the land between the Mediterranean and the Jordan river, all in one color and marks the location of roads, cities, and bodies of water throughout the area as if the whole space were fully integrated and open across infrastructures. What it does not do is show the occupied Palestinian territories as distinct from the rest of the map. The border between the West Bank and Israel is barely visible, and it is not labelled. It also replaces Palestinian names for towns, regions, and natural features with ancient, Biblical names. The West Bank becomes Judea and Samaria for example.

Maps can be politically charged documents. The worst maps *lie* about the world to support a political position or to advance an oppressive strategy. One of Ariel Sharon's trademark images was to stand in front of his jeep, parked somewhere in occupied territory, map spread out on the hood, studying, or illustrating something from the map and pointing to the land. These pictures of Sharon, the strategic pioneer, cast both his involvement in the early Israel settlement project and again, with the process of mapping out the route for the separation barrier. The second map is in this category. It is a piece of propaganda that assumes and entrenches the blindness of its readers to the existence of the Occupied Palestinian Territories (OPT): the West Bank, East Jerusalem, and Gaza strip. The political message behind the map is that these territories *are* part of Israel, that Israel is incomplete without the OPT, that those who insist that Palestine and Palestinians exist and have the right to self-determination are in fact mistaken.

The "lie" that this map tells is not someone else's lie. In a way, it has been my lie, a falsehood that my country and my religious community have accepted and reinforced about what is happening in Israel and Palestine. The map is merely one product of a much larger issue of the lack of consciousness of one community on one side of the

Atlantic to the existence and struggles of another community, under military occupation, on the other side of the ocean. Throughout the project, in the back of my mind, I have had to keep track of the moral difference between Sharon's interest in maps and my own.

Findings

The research processes I described generated a range of findings. This section presents the following results. Physical descriptions of occupation, settler colonial, and educational spaces are presented. Three maps are also included, each at different scales, to situate Bethlehem and Bethlehem's campuses in their spatial context, with particular attention to occupation and settler colonial space. Images of key infrastructures and campus spaces are presented to illustrate the particularities of educational and infrastructural spaces.

The mapping work and direct observation allowed me to produce a series of spatial artifacts such as maps and images. The following sections present spatial themes that emerged from this work, weaving together maps, images, and narratives to illustrate these findings.

Roads and Tunnels

Northbound from the checkpoint, Highway 60 (known as the *tunnel road* locally) plunges twice into tunnels and serves as an express route for settlement traffic directly to and from Jerusalem (Figure 11). Between the tunnels, the separation barrier flanks the highway on both sides to control access to the road and protect the Israeli traffic from the Palestinian areas through which it is built. This infrastructure simultaneously hems in development of the Bethlehem/Beit Jala/Beit Sahour district and excludes West Bank Palestinians from using the road north of the checkpoint. The highlighted color fields

Figure 11

Bypass Road to the Northwest Side of Beit Jala

Note: The areas on both sides of the highway, the foreground, and the other side of the valley between the separation barrier and the settlements are western parts of the Bethlehem District.

highlight space that is only available for use by those with Israeli license plates (lower image, Figure 11).

Highway 375 originates near the al Khadr intersection at the southwest edge of the Bethlehem District and runs west through the West Bank and into Israel. Palestinians are required to have a special permit to use this road. The road connects Israeli settlement, Better Illit, the Highway 60 (known by locals as the *Tunnel Road*) which serves as a major artery through the West Bank and into Jerusalem. Students at the institutions that participated in this study use the Palestinian road (highlighted green in Figures 12 & 13) to commute to their campuses. Highway 375 is depicted in Figures 12 and 13 with pink highlighting, and the road designated for Palestinian traffic is highlighted in green. This is an example of an intersection that is not an intersection, a bridge with no entrance or exit ramps. This infrastructure enables Israeli settlement

Figure 12

On the Palestinian Road to Nahalin, Passing Under the Israeli Road to Betar Illit

Figure 13

Google Maps Screenshot of the Same Intersection, on Highway 375 From Betar Illit, Passing Over the Road From Nahalin

[Figure: highway photograph with legend showing "Israeli road" and "Palestinian road, Bethlehem to Nahalin"]

populations to commute in and out of the West Bank while minimizing exposure to Palestinian traffic. When a road that Palestinians can use enters a Palestinian area, the threshold is marked by a standard sign that states in Hebrew, Arabic, and English, "This road leads to area 'A' under the Palestinian Authority. Entrance for Israeli Citizens is forbidden. Dangerous to your lives and is against the Israeli law" (Figure 14).

The Separation Barrier (Also Known as the Apartheid Wall)

A high concrete wall cuts across the northern and western extremities of the Bethlehem district (which includes the town of Bethlehem, as well as Beit Jala to the West and Beit Sahour to the east). A political border, the concrete separation barrier (Figure 15), and multiple Israeli colonial settlements (Figure 10) are squeezed into the handful of kilometers between Jerusalem and Bethlehem. To look at a map of Bethlehem that includes both political borders and infrastructure is to be struck by a dazzling array

Figure 14

Standard Sign at Entrances to Palestinian Areas (Area A) in the West Bank

Figure 15

Separation Barrier With Sniper Tower Near Checkpoint 300. Picture by Author

Note: The separation barrier and sniper tower as it passes across the northern boundary of Bethlehem near Bethlehem Bible College and Aida Camp (refugee camp in northern Bethlehem).

of overlapping lines, zones, borders, and infrastructures. In 1949, when the war concluded, the parties drew an armistice line (the *green line*). This is the political boundary for what came to be known as the West Bank (so called because it is on the West bank of the Jordan River). This line ran through Jerusalem, dividing West from East, before turning and proceeding East-West along the far southern edge of Jerusalem. The green line was multiple kilometers north of Bethlehem. In the early 2000s, when Israel began building its separation barrier, the authorities placed the 9-meter-high concrete wall deeply inside of the West Bank as it passed Bethlehem, de facto annexing Bethlehem's northern hinterlands to Israel. The land between the green line and the separation barrier is politically part of the West Bank but is on the Israeli side of the wall. These areas are called the *seam zone*. As it passes near checkpoint 300, the wall makes a diving incision into the upper heart of Bethlehem to enclose the traditional burial site of the tomb of the Biblical matriarch, Rachel, on the Israeli side of the wall. The wall proceeds tightly around the western border of Beit Jala, Bethlehem's neighbor to the West, before curling around part of the southern extremity of town. The wall contains and prevents development of Bethlehem on two sides. Israeli settlements, Gilo, Har Gilo, Har Homa, and Efrat surround Bethlehem to the north and south. As the wall continues outside of the built-up area of Bethlehem, the materials used for the wall change to razor wire (Figure 16).

Checkpoints

There are gates and checkpoints placed in the wall at certain points. These gates allow Israeli authorities to control movement from one side of the gate to the other. Today, there are two main approaches to Bethlehem from Jerusalem: Checkpoint 300,

Figure 16

The Separation Barrier is Coiled Barbed Wire and Razor Wire in Rural Areas. Image Taken Near al-Walaja. Picture Taken by the Author

which is known for long lines of pedestrians and vehicle traffic, and a multi-lane checkpoint for vehicle traffic at the bottom of the hill below Beit Jala on Highway 60. At these checkpoints, soldiers stop, check, turn back, and conduct other regulatory actions toward Palestinians who wish to pass. I often took the bus to Jerusalem through the Highway 60 checkpoint when I stayed in Bethlehem. The bus stopped at the checkpoint each time I went to Jerusalem—never on the way back. When we stopped, Palestinians would disembark and stand in a line next to the bus while Israeli soldiers boarded, checked paperwork for those with Israeli and other IDs, then disembarked to check the Palestinians' IDs and entry permits separately before allowing the Palestinians back on the bus. On one occasion the soldiers pulled a woman off the bus, and we left without her.

Refugee Camps

Bethlehem is also the site of multiple urban refugee camps, Aida Camp (Figure 17) and Beit Jebrin Camp in the northern part of town and Dheisheh Camp in the southern part of town. Originally built for the Palestinian refugees fleeing the Jewish militias in 1948, several generations later, the population density in these camps now can be higher than that of New York City. Hebron Road, a main artery running diagonally along the border between Bethlehem and Beit Jala, has multi-story commercial and retail buildings along certain stretches—banks, stores, and offices mostly—before proceeding past Dheisheh Camp and south out of town on its way to Hebron. Historic Bethlehem lies

Figure 17

From Inside the Gate to Aida Refugee Camp, Looking Up at a Gate in the Separation Barrier, a Site for Frequent Clashes. Picture Taken by the Author.

Note: On the other side of the gate in the wall at the top of the hill is the historic shrine to the Biblical Matriarch Rachel. Soldiers who come out of that gate during clashes will have passed directly beside the shrine.

up the hill east of Hebron Road. Because the separation barrier runs along the northern edge of Aida camp, tensions associated with the wall and with the camp tend to concentrate there. There is a gate in the wall in line of site with one of the main entrances to the camp (Figure 17)—this location is a frequent site for clashes between refugees and Israeli soldiers. This area is close to higher education spaces in Bethlehem (Figure 18). Palestinians may demonstrate or throw rocks and Israeli soldiers may fire rubber bullets and tear gas (Figures 19 and 20 show used rubber bullets and tear gas canisters picked up in the camp). In fact, a Palestinian teenager was shot and killed there. Because of the proximity to the wall, there is also a sniper tower adjacent to the camp with lines of sight along key roads to the interior of the camp. In general, refugees do not have the same status with the municipality as their neighbors and do not have the same access to municipal services such as waste management, water, and electricity.

Figure 18

Panorama From Aida Refugee Camp Facing Northeast. Picture Taken by the Author

Figure 19

Rubber Bullets Picked Up in Aida Refugee Camp After They Were Used Against Residents. Picture Taken by the Author

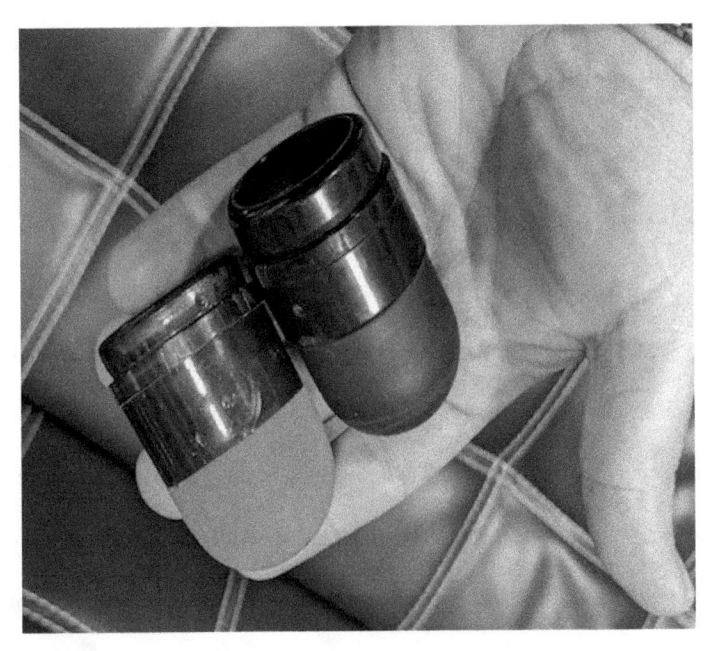

Figure 20

Used Tear Gas Canister Picked Up in Aida Refugee Camp. Picture Taken by the Author

Surrounding Communities

The Bethlehem district serves as a center of Palestinian activity in the Bethlehem Governorate and is connected through these activities to surrounding Palestinian villages and cities including al-Walaja, Nahalin, Husan and to cities beyond the governorate such as Hebron to the south. Some of these communities ended up on the same side of the separation barrier with Bethlehem, others on the other side. These communities exist in their own spatial configurations of Israeli infrastructure. Al-Walaja (Figures 21 and 22), for example, is bordered directly by the separation barrier, and its residents face a uniquely high threat of home demolitions (Figure 23). Al-Walaja was included in the areas Israel de facto annexed in 1980, yet it is on the West Bank side of the wall, so its residents do not have the same access to Jerusalem services or support. One family described in an interview that Israeli authorities had demolished their home, arriving in the middle of the night with multiple bulldozers and dozens of soldiers present to protect

Figure 21

Panorama Above the Palestinian Town al-Walaja. Picture Taken by the Author

Figure 22

Separation Barrier as It Passes Between al-Walaja and Its Properties. Picture Taken by the Author

the bulldozers as they destroyed their home. Following the demolition, the family (husband, wife, and two young children), lived in a shipping container placed on their land. A few years later, they were able to rebuild their home, where they live now, but owe Israel fees that exceed the equivalent of 200,000 U.S. dollars for building without a permit. Because these fees are past due, they are unable to pass checkpoints because they would risk being arrested. The ways infrastructures of control are configured can be different from space to space. Efforts to expand Israeli presence in the greater Eastern Jerusalem area include Israeli settlement the Old City of Jerusalem, including in Arab and Christian quarters, and settlement initiatives in neighborhoods such as Silwan and Sheikh Jarrah.

Figure 23

Ruins of a Palestinian Home Demolished by Israeli Authorities in al Walaja. Picture Taken by the Author

Campuses

There are multiple colleges and universities in this area (Figure 24), including Bethlehem University which has a walled campus with white stone buildings, stone paths, and a courtyard with garden surrounded by residential streets north of Manger Square. Since Bethlehem University is located on a hill, there are views all around, including a view of the nearby Israeli settlement, Har Homa (Figures 25 & 26). Bethlehem Bible College is a smaller institution at the northern end of town with a campus on Hebron Road, a stone's throw from Checkpoint 300. Dar Al-Kalima University College of Arts and Culture is further south, tucked into a neighborhood east

119

Figure 24

Institutions of Higher Learning Relative to the Wall and Checkpoint. Map by Author

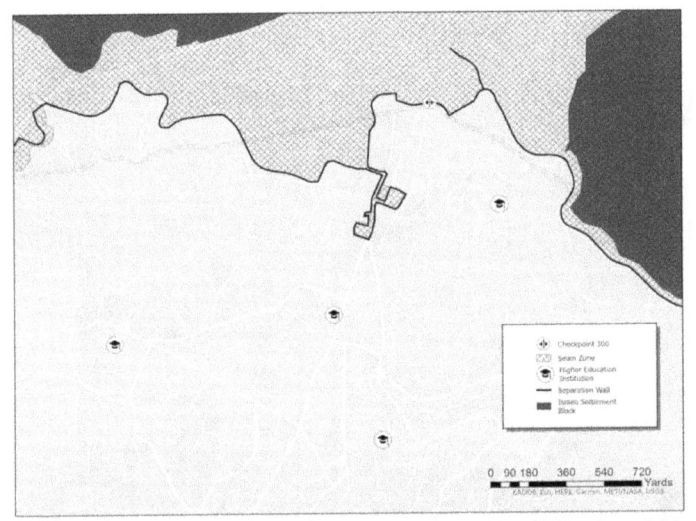

Note: Dar al-Kalima University is located further south off the edge of this map.

Figure 25

View From Bethlehem University Northeast to Israeli Settlement Har Homa. Picture Taken by the Author

Figure 26

View From Bethlehem University Northeast to Israeli Settlement Har Homa With Highlights. Picture Taken by the Author

of Hebron Road and close to the northern edge of Dheisheh Camp. Palestine Ahliya University borders Dar Al-Kalima to the Southwest.

Spatial Locations and Educational Implications

Residential location and status determine much about which challenges a Palestinian will face in pursuing education at the tertiary level. Groups of Palestinians can be differentiated by where they live and by legal status (see Figure 27):

1. West Bank resident with Palestinian Authority passport
2. Living in the West Bank but holding no legal ID
3. Residents of East Jerusalem
4. Palestinian/Arab citizens of Israel (who hold an Israeli passport)

5. Palestinians in diaspora (who live outside of the Palestinian territories and outside of Israel)
6. Refugees in the West Bank
7. Refugees outside of the West Bank

Each category carries with it subcategories and permutations that can also affect access to education or nature of the access, particularly where spatial zones and/or legal statuses overlap with each other. For example, the Jerusalem municipality extends in certain

Figure 27

Bethlehem Relative to Closure Points and Area C. Map Created by the Author

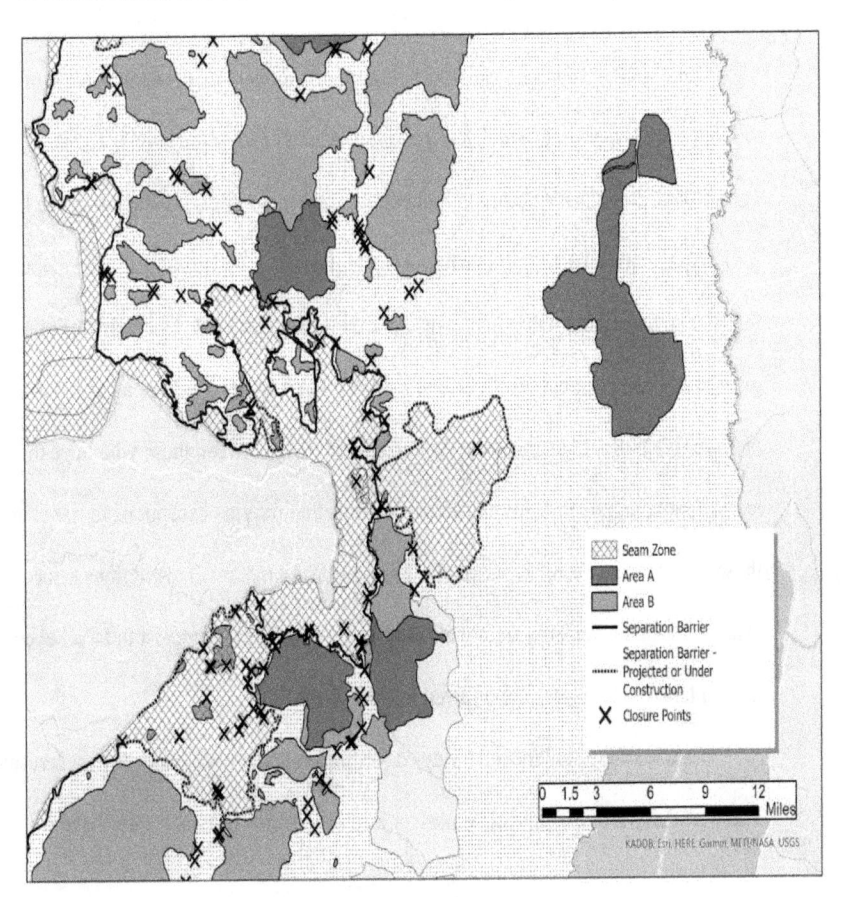

points across the separation barrier to the *West Bank side* of the wall such that Palestinians living in these areas are residents of Jerusalem, but usually without municipal services (because of the wall) and may experience the heightened pressure on their residency that is characteristic of Israeli policy in Palestinian neighborhoods throughout East Jerusalem. Near Bethlehem, the town of al Walaja is one such place. A few thousand live on a hilltop directly adjacent to an Israeli settlement to the east and tightly bounded by the separation barrier to the north. At least one of the universities in this study have multiple students enrolled in 2022 from al Walaja.

Participants in this study include members of multiple categories, but especially residents of the West Bank, residents of East Jerusalem, and refugees in the West Bank. Those with a West Bank passport are not normally allowed to leave the West Bank without a special permit, which has a range of educational implications. These Palestinians do not have access to higher education institutions in Israel or in the Israeli settlements in the West Bank (such as Ariel University). The growth and development that can be associated with visiting new places is also curtailed. The reality of this group gives rise to the popular description of the West Bank by its residents as an *open-air prison*. This policy also creates a socioeconomic filter between those who have the means and wherewithal to apply for and secure permits that provide exceptions to travel and those who do not. There are curricular implications to the travel restrictions—for example, tourism students are not allowed to travel to sites of interest in Israel even though Israeli tour guides are allowed into the West Bank.

Many of the students interviewed for this project are residents of East Jerusalem. These students are residents of Jerusalem, but not citizens of Israel. They have a residential status in Israel, thus, they commute from Jerusalem (which Israel considers to be in its state) into the West Bank to attend college. To make this commute, they pass through Checkpoint 300 on their way to and from campus. Passage through the checkpoint can be an embarrassing or stressful experience given the direct engagement with Israeli soldiers and potential for unpredictable interactions. The amount of time it takes is also unpredictable. In some cases, Israeli policy prevents people from carrying certain kinds of educational materials or tools through the checkpoint (faculty mentioned certain kinds of tools used by ceramics students for example that have been confiscated at this checkpoint). In these cases, students must leave their tools on campus, or they may be taken at the checkpoint.

One of the institutions in Bethlehem shared residential location data for their currently enrolled students (academic year 2021-2022). Figure 28 indicates the percentage of their student body from each governorate in the West Bank. Based on the figure, the highest percentage of students enrolled are from the Bethlehem governorate (67.9%). The next highest percentage come from East Jerusalem (13.4%) and then the Hebron governorate (12.8%). Then the numbers drop off precipitously with Ramallah governorate supplying 3.7% of the student body and less than 1% from any other area in the West Bank. These findings resonate with the interview data that describe how difficult it is for students from the north to enroll in Bethlehem institutions since the separation barrier started to be built. Another way to understand residential data is to log the locations where students live (Figures 29 & 30). By gathering this data, it is possible to analyze the commutes that would be required for students to arrive on campus.

Figure 28

Percentage of Student Body Residential Locations by Governorate From a Participating Institution in Bethlehem

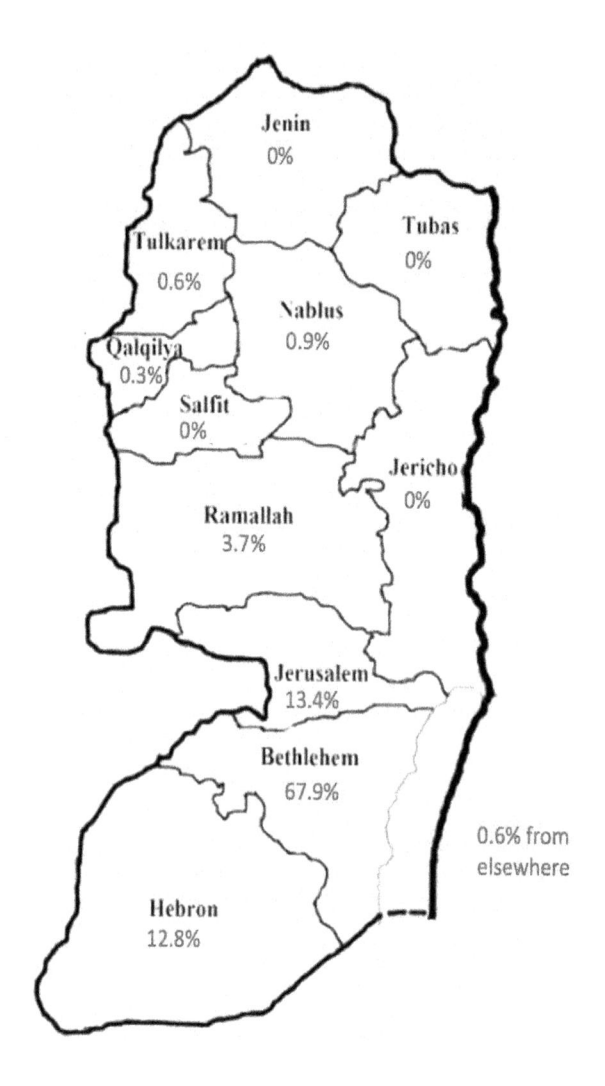

Figure 29

Localities of Residence of Currently Enrolled Students at a Single Institution in Bethlehem. Map Created by the Author

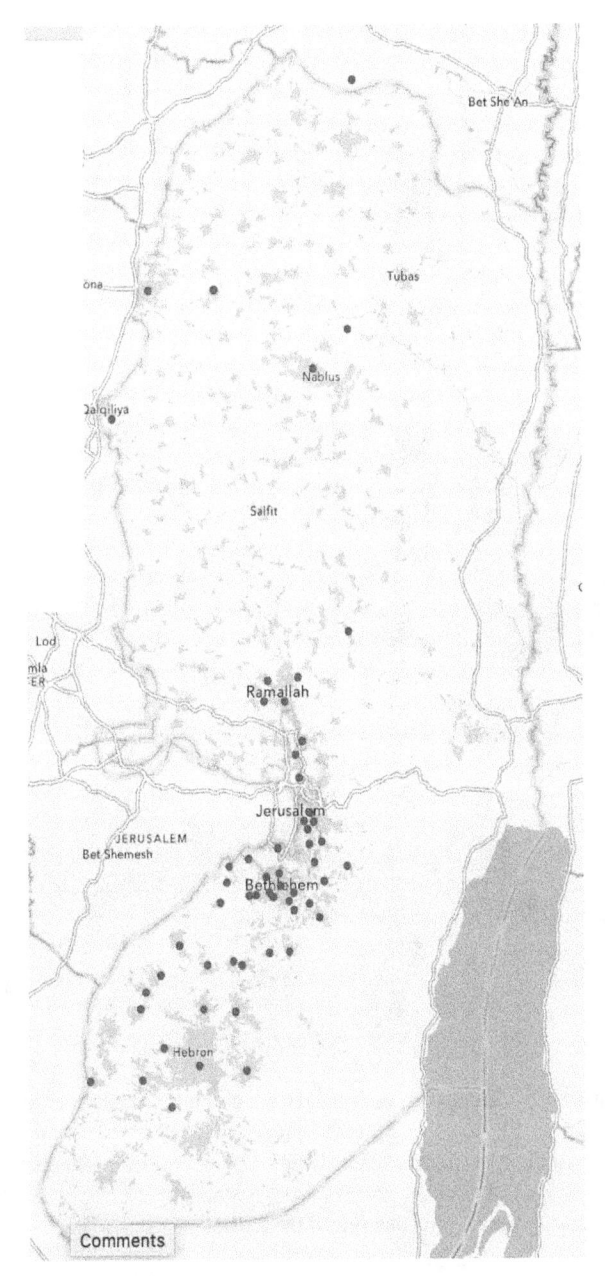

Figure 30

Same Figure as Figure 29 but with Oslo Areas A, B, and C Overlaid. Map Created by the Author.

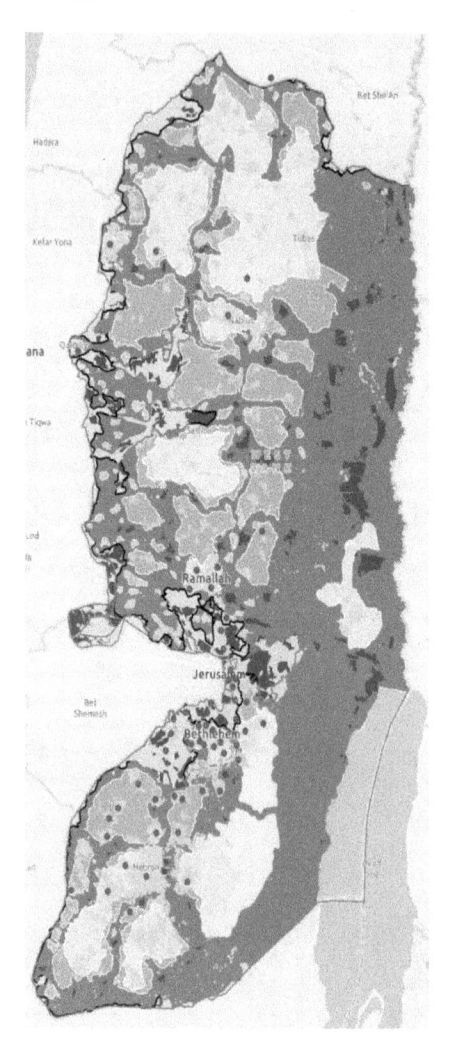

The real number of students from each geographic area also demonstrates the geographic fracturing of the educational market (Figure 31). Parts of East Jerusalem, comprising much of the grey area, is on one side of the separation barrier. The implications of being from north of Jerusalem or south, in East Jerusalem or in other places is highlighted by this figure. These implications range from where prospective students will consider enrolling, what their commutes will be like (or whether they will have to try to find housing in a new city), and what zones or checkpoints they will have to pass regularly.

Checkpoints

Virtually all participants shared stories about their students who have faced direct, harsh, encounters with Israeli policies and Israeli soldiers. Students have been detained by soldiers, deported from the West Bank, shot, and placed under house arrest. One

Figure 31

Number of Students by Residential Location Currently Enrolled at a Participating Institution

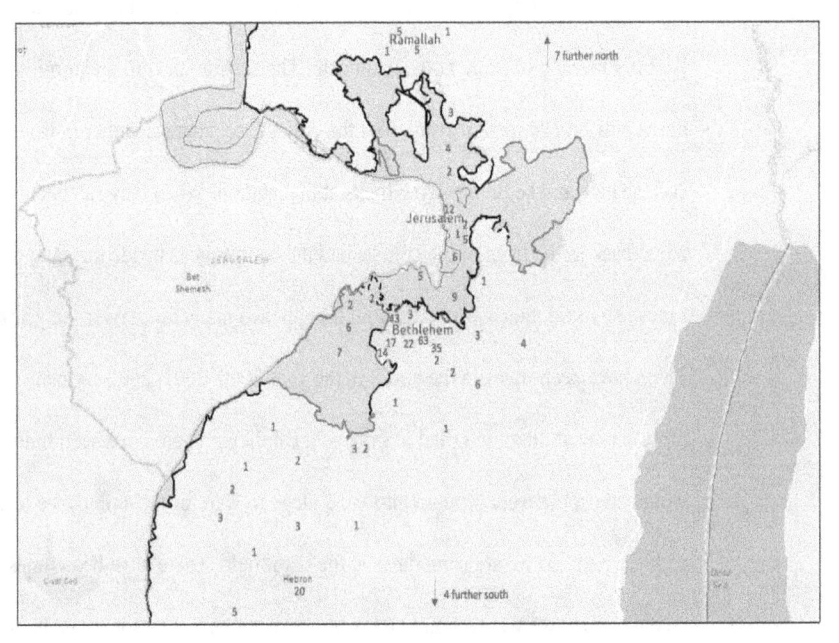

participant described a tearful meeting with a student whose home near Hebron was demolished by Israeli forces and whose family had to move north to Ramallah. This student was unable to finish her studies in Bethlehem and had to unenroll in a university in a new city. Another shared about a young female student who was placed under "obliged residency" (house arrest) after Israeli forces detained her at a political demonstration in East Jerusalem. She missed her classes for the rest of the semester.

One of the institutions represented by participants in this study is located near a main checkpoint where Palestinians regularly stage demonstrations. As a result, demonstrations and clashes with Israeli soldiers happen on the street directly in front of this campus. A leader from this institution explained:

> Many times, the demonstrations against the Israeli occupation happen in front of the college because we have an Israeli checkpoint nearby, so the experience of teargas and shooting in front of [name of institution] is something we got used to [...] It's literally in front, at the main gate. The separation wall under military bases may be 100 meters away from the college, so students gather in front of the college gate and begin throwing rocks at that station. When they run back, they come back to the front of the college and the teargas goes inside the campus many times. As I said, that's very common. It happened many times over the years [...] There have been times in the past—in the year 2000, 2001, 2002—when protesters were literally killed in front of the college. There have been times when wounded people were brought into the college to wait for the ambulance to come pick them up, so we are sometimes at the battlefield. There have been times recently when we would simply know in advance, and using social media, we

> would move the location. We would go to another institute and stay there especially for evening classes. We've done that many times. […] If the class is at 4 and the demonstration begins at 2, we send a message that the class is going to take place usually in a church. We'd go to a church because of safety.

The experiences this leader was describing highlight the principal roles location and geography play in Palestine. A campus located near a checkpoint will experience the tensions attendant with such a checkpoint. In fact, when asked about ways the Israeli occupation impacted students, participants talked about checkpoints more than any other challenge. The institutions in this study are located in Bethlehem, which is close to Jerusalem (downtown Bethlehem is 6 miles from downtown Jerusalem), but since Bethlehem is in the West Bank, and Jerusalem is in Israel proper, Palestinian students who live in East Jerusalem encounter this checkpoint twice each day, once on the way and once on the way back. There are countless internal checkpoints inside the West Bank as well, so travelling between cities and villages inside of the West Bank also often requires passing through one or more checkpoints. Participants repeatedly connected checkpoints to encounters with Israeli soldiers, violence, student trauma, and loss of time in class. Because encounters with soldiers can increase risks and costs to Palestinian students and soldiers are concentrated at checkpoints, these can be sites of violence, humiliation, and trauma for Palestinian students and faculty. One participant mentioned that students have had friends shot at checkpoints and another that students have been detained at checkpoints. One participant shared about a student's recent experience:

> I remember I was shocked one day when one of my students said that on her way to the university, one of the soldiers who went on the bus to check their IDs

pointed the gun in her face. I was shocked. She was laughing. She was laughing because she was used to it. She had seen it many times. When you talk to the students about the way they are treated at the checkpoints...I heard them talk about how they feel less than human when they are treated that way. It's a dehumanizing, humiliating experience. But these kids are very resilient.

Again, this experience highlights the outsized role checkpoints play in the daily lives of educators and students. In addition to risk of violence and trauma, participants also talked about logistical challenges checkpoints pose to students. Because of the long lines that can suddenly develop at checkpoints, students can miss class time because they were delayed at a checkpoint. By the same token, they can lose study time. Participants also talked about the impact of checkpoints and the associated system of travel permits on some students' ability to register for field trips, study tours, and service teams. One institution takes student teams to volunteer among Syrian refugees in Jordan—but some students are unable to participate because they cannot secure travel permits to leave the West Bank. "It's very challenging for them to rely on the goodwill of the military and everything that they have to do in traveling from one place to another" as one participant put it, "On the ground, life can be very complicated. It's very hard to plan for events. It's very hard to physically move from one place to another." This quote points to some of the implications for higher education when basic mobility is unpredictable for students and employees.

Because goods are subject to search and confiscation at checkpoints, students whose programs require specialized equipment face further challenges. For example, sculpture students are unable to carry their specialized equipment like glass cutters to work at home—as a result, they often stay late at school to work on their sculptures on campus, where the institution provides lockers to keep their tools. One participant estimated that 15% of the student body at his institution are residents of Jerusalem and pass through Checkpoint 300 each day.

Several participants talked about the unique impact checkpoints used to have on students from Gaza. Israel prohibits Gazan students from traveling to the West Bank, but they used to come to enroll in college. When that was the case, these students had to stay in Bethlehem and avoid checkpoints where their presence in the West Bank would be noticed by Israeli forces. One participant told a story about a student who was a month from graduation. She traveled to Ramallah for a job interview but was stopped at a checkpoint and deported and missed her last month of classes and her graduation.

Discussion

This study demonstrates that in Bethlehem, higher education campuses are part of a landscape that includes occupation and settler-colonial infrastructures including a separation barrier, checkpoints, militarization, bypass roads, and other infrastructures of spatial control and apartheid. Together, these infrastructures serve as a kind of machinery that separates populations from each other in the same land and sorts them into designated zones. The machinery systematically resources, mobilizes, and connects one population and simultaneously denies, demobilizes, and isolates the other population. Furthermore, this machinery and its attendant policies create challenges that Palestinian educators and learners must account for as they practice educational and learning-related activities. The campuses studied in this project each have walls surrounding all or most campus buildings. These walls are normative for many kinds of properties and buildings in Bethlehem, yet they are also helpful for separating educational space from the surrounding environment, from the machinery that enwraps the lives of educators and learners.

Spatio-Epistemics

This study suggests the way space is inhabited influences how knowledge can be nurtured. Space is necessary to the development and the preservation of a range of types of knowledge. It might seem strange to think about space as regulating knowledge when the Internet is so widely available regardless of political and physical borders. But of course, knowledge is much bigger and more diverse than the kind of information that can be conveyed through the Internet. To be sure, knowledge conducted via the Internet still requires spatial access to a computer or smart phone as well as electrical and communications infrastructure, which is not necessarily available in remote areas and should not be taken for granted. But raw information is only one kind of knowledge. Being aware of information is different from knowing a person, knowing oneself, knowing one's home, knowing one's family, knowing one's livelihood, knowing one's heritage, and knowing one's land. These embodied forms of knowing are relational and place-based in ways that are impacted by imposed spatial configurations. For purposes of this study, I use the term *spatio-epistemic* to highlight these relationships between space and knowledge.

The themes highlighted in this study—the fracturing of Palestinian educational space and the educational experiences of Palestinians in that spatial landscape—suggest provisional relationships between types of knowledge and the spatial modes required for their development (Table 1). When students spend time in a place (*presence*) such as

Table 1

Spatial Modalities and Corresponding Types of Knowledge

Spatial Mode:	Knowledge Types:
Presence	Familiarity - recognizability that arises from a long and close acquaintance
Practice	Facility - skilled ability to perform complex activities
Formal study	Formal expertise - knowledge authorized by recognized credentialing authorities
Archeology	Rootedness - bonds to the land that arise from mutual belonging

Note. This table presents provisional relationships between types of knowledge and the spatial modes that may facilitate their nurture.

their home, the homes of relatives, or public parks, they develop a special kind of *familiarity* with that space that is different than the kind of knowledge that comes from reading a book or looking at a map. When students conduct an experiment in a lab (*practice*), they develop a kind of skilled muscle memory (*facility*) that differs from the knowledge that comes from a lecture. When students attend classes at educational institutions (*formal study*), they can acquire an official credential establishing their social authority in a given area of knowledge (*formal expertise*). When archeologists unearth artifacts and structures in underground space, and when stories about people are connected to these artifacts, knowledge about historic presence can be nurtured (*rootedness*).

Some of these spatio-epistemic connections are plain enough to be taken for granted, especially by those whose use of space is facilitated. The described relationships may not be unique to Palestine, but the ways spatial practices are controlled *is* distinctive. This study suggests spatial control in the Bethlehem district may have knowledge effects that must be navigated by residents.

In the digital age when the Internet is so broadly available, access to information is available like never-before in history, and walls and checkpoints are largely irrelevant to the flow of this kind of information. But other, more embodied forms of knowing are more deeply affected by physical infrastructures that control the use of space. This study suggests provisional relations between space and knowledge mediated by *how the space is configured*, whether the spatial configuration inhibits knowledge-producing uses of space (Table 2). For example, the forced evacuation of people from land (*barrier/ checkpoint*) impacts the kinds of knowledge of these lands (*familiarity*) that are possible among these populations. Preventing students of tourism studies programs from traveling in the Holy Land outside of the West Bank (*barrier/checkpoints*) limits their access to familiarity with the holy sites (*familiarity and facility*). Preventing imports of lab resources for STEM programs impacts the development of skills that require practice. Given the suggested relations between spatial modes and types of knowledge, epistemic implications follow. For example, the separation barrier, which prevents mobility, also prevents familiarity. It prevents West Bank Palestinians from being present in many areas, thus preventing them from developing familiarity with these areas. Import restrictions, which restrict what supplies, materials, and equipment can be imported into the West Bank, regulate acquisition, which regulates practice. For example, the

Table 2

Settler Colonial Mechanisms and Spatio-Epistemic Functions

Machinery Components	Spatial function	Epistemic function
Barrier	Prevents mobility	Prevents familiarity, prevents spatial practices
Checkpoint/gate	Regulates mobility	Regulates familiarity
Import restrictions	Prevents acquisition	Prevents practices
Home demolitions	Removes residents	Destabilizes rootedness

restriction on chemicals that need to be used for developing film, means Palestinian art students cannot practice certain darkroom techniques. The restriction on chemicals used for cleaning metals in jewelry-making prevents the development of core experiences.

This study does not address ways Palestinian educational practices may respond to the physical and epistemic challenges described herein. It leaves open the question: How do Palestinian educators and learners in higher education navigate and resist the challenges related to physical and epistemic navigation of these landscapes? If appropriation is the opposite of domination, then how do Palestinian educators appropriate the elements of their moment, of their social and spatial world? And what is the aim of these appropriations? Do they seek to create places for dwelling and development, as Lefebvre (1992) articulated is the proper aim of the family home? There is reason, from conversations with Palestinian educators, to suggest at least some of them do seek, nearly as precisely as could be, to do just that, to make their students' space that is free from immediate threat, free from overwhelming existential distractions, for students to learn, to explore, to develop, and to send roots into the ground. The next article addresses these questions.

CHAPTER 4

HOUSE OF BREAD: PALESTINIAN HIGHER EDUCATION IN BETHLEHEM

Palestinian senior spokesperson, Hanan Ashrawi was born in 1940s Palestine to politically active parents. In her book, Ashrawi (1996) recalled national political heroes regularly coming in and out of her home for political meetings and personal visits. She grew up where the action was, where the efforts for Palestinian self-determination and visions for statehood were most clearly and lovingly articulated and nurtured. As Ashrawi grew, she began to participate and gain influence in this political community. After the Israelis occupied the West Bank in 1967, these became secret meetings. They met in people's living rooms and on their rooftops over meals and cigarettes, but always with precautions. Early in the book, Ashrawi described the anguish of waiting for news of her family from her college campus in Beirut as the Israelis invaded the West Bank, not knowing whether her family was alive. This experience, she wrote, marked a turning point after which she took personal ownership of the political vision and energy of her family. It is this vision and energy she's exercised for nearly 60 years in the cause of Palestinian self-determination as a public figure, as a political leader, and as an academic at one of Palestine's premier universities.

During her tenure as a dean at Birzeit University, Ashrawi had countless confrontations with the Israeli occupation forces. When Ashrawi was there, Birzeit students and faculty were politically active and regularly staged demonstrations against the occupation. In her book, Ashrawi (1996) described opening campus gates to let students stream back onto the walled campus as Israeli soldiers pursued them, seeking to suppress the demonstrations. With tear gas in the air, Ashrawi would close the gate with students safely inside and stand alone outside the gate, between her students and the soldiers. On other occasions, Ashrawi was the intended target of Israeli bullets—she kept a collection of the casings of these bullets until she was invited to join the Palestinian peace process. In many ways—her political resistance as a professor, the political engagement of her students, the role of intellectualism against the occupation, the direct application of force against faculty and students, the incursions onto campus, the detentions of intellectuals—Ashrawi's stories typify higher education in Palestine in the 1970s and 1980s.

The Oslo process, a series of negotiations between Israel and a group of Palestinians in the early 1990s, changed the structure of the occupation, and with it, the structure and roles of Palestinian higher education. The Oslo process instituted the Palestinian Authority, the proto government that was intended to become the government of a future Palestinian state (Bauck & Omer, 2017). The plan placed the administration of higher education under the Palestinian Authority. Oslo also instituted a geographical regime that fractured Palestinian space into separate enclaves which has had far reaching implications for all Palestinian institutions, including Palestinian colleges and universities (PCUs; Bauck & Omer, 2017). The occupation since Oslo has been marked by economic exploitation (Al-Haq, 2015), restriction of physical mobility (Applied Research Institute – Jerusalem, 2017; Tawile-Souri, 2011), geographic fracturing (Monaghan & Careccia, 2012; Peteet, 2017)), infrastructural exploitation (Koek, 2013; Meiton, 2019), and an ongoing Israeli settlement project (Veracini, 2006); thus, the occupation has functioned as an enforcement mechanism for a creeping settler colonial transfer of Israeli civilians into the West Bank and displacement of Palestinian communities into dense urban areas (Khalidi, 2007). PCUs have faced unique challenges, opportunities, and pressures while operating under these conditions (Baramki, 2010; Jebril, 2018). This chapter seeks to contribute to a deeper understanding of the role of higher education in a Palestinian city in the West Bank in relationship to the Israeli occupation and settler colonial project. The goal driving this article is to develop a richly descriptive exploration of Palestinian higher education in Bethlehem, one of the Palestinian enclaves in the West Bank. On a conceptual level, this chapter is an attempt to explore the nature of the impacts of the occupation on Palestinian higher education and how Palestinian educators and students respond in efforts to pursue quality education, learning, and research.

Literature

This section includes a brief history of Israel's occupation of the West Bank, a more focused review of post-Oslo conditions, a summary of the current structure of the Palestinian higher education system, a geographic description of Bethlehem, and a review of settler colonial theory.

Present Higher Education System

PCUs operate across various geographies, performing different functions for diverse constituencies. Most of the largest Palestinian population centers have one or more institutions including Ramallah, Nablus, Jenin, Bethlehem, Jericho, Hebron, and Gaza City. Major institutions include An Najah University in Nablus, Birzeit University outside of Ramallah, Al Quds University on multiple campuses in East Jerusalem and Abu Dies, Bethlehem University in Bethlehem, Hebron Polytechnic University in Hebron, and Al Azhar University in Gaza. There are also a whole range of small and medium size institutions. Across the system, institutions offer a range of educational options in medicine, law, natural sciences, humanities, technology, security, teacher training, and broader, liberal arts tracks as well (Ministry of Education and Higher Education, 2013; RecoNow, 2016).

The Palestinian Ministry of Education and Higher Education recognizes four categories of higher education: universities (containing three or more colleges and conferring graduate degrees), university colleges (conferring 2-, 3-, 4-year degrees), polytechnic colleges (conferring vocational certificates and degrees), and community colleges (certificates and associates degrees in mid-level professional fields). There are currently 51 PCUs operating in the West Bank (including East Jerusalem) and Gaza (Ministry of Higher Education and Scientific Research, 2021). These institutions include 16 traditional universities, 16 university colleges, 17 community colleges (as well as a handful of technical training institutes which the Ministry of Education and Higher Education does not count as PCUs), and two open universities. The estimated national enrollment in 2021 was 214,765 students across all institutions, which is roughly a quarter of the college-age cohort in Palestine (Ministry of Higher Education and Scientific Research, 2021). To enroll in a Palestinian college or university, students must secure their General Secondary Education Certificate (*Tawjihi*). Doing so typically requires students to complete at least 12 years of education before entering college, 10 of which are compulsory (RecoNow, 2016).

Post-Oslo Conditions

The Oslo peace agreements of the 1990s divided the West Bank into three, non-contiguous zones, each ostensibly governed by a different configuration of Palestinian and Israeli authorities (Applied Research Institute – Jerusalem, 2017; Shafir, 2017). Israel has imposed a regime of military checkpoints and ethnic identity cards to control and surveil Palestinian movement in the West Bank (Berda, 2018; Peteet, 2017; Tawil-Souri, 2011)—there are over 250 checkpoints throughout the West Bank designed to control pedestrian or motor traffic. Checkpoints can be characterized by long lines and unpredictable policy changes (Berda, 2018; Monaghan & Careccia, 2012; Sfard, 2018), creating exceptionally long and circuitous commutes for Palestinians, and can extend travel distances by multiple times. Thus, this system sufficiently disincentivizes travel for many Palestinians, such that some simply refuse to venture beyond their township, seeking to avoid the inconvenience, embarrassment, and even danger that can attend passage through checkpoints.

The settlement of Israelis in the West Bank is considered illegal under international law (Shehadeh, 1985)—article 49 of the Fourth Geneva Convention (1949) articulates that "The Occupying Power shall not deport or transfer parts of its own civilian population into the territory it occupies." Nevertheless, Israel continues to facilitate and protect the expansion of existing settlements and the construction of new settlements (Monaghan & Careccia, 2012), expropriating Palestinian land and compromising the geographic contiguity of Palestinian communities. In addition to the accumulation of families, Israeli organizations are also building public institutions in the settlements, including a university. Ariel University currently enrolls 16,000 students, most of whom commute from Israel proper via an Israeli-only freeway inside the West Bank. By 2017, there were 131 illegal settlements throughout the Palestinian West Bank, not including unsanctioned outpost communities (B'Tselem, 2019).

Since the PCUs were established after the occupation began, these institutions have grown and adapted under conditions in which they had to account for the presence and force of the Israeli military and other occupation entities. For example, colleges and universities have been subject to military orders (Audeh, 2017; Baramki, 1987; Sullivan, 1991). Under Order 854, issued in 1980, Israel claimed broad powers over many aspects of the Palestinian academy (Baramki, 2010; Jerusalem Media and Communications Center, 1990; Sullivan, 1991), including the right to block students from enrolling and to withhold teaching permits from faculty. PCUs have experienced a variety of other challenges and indignities from Israeli authorities, including arrests of students, faculty, and administration (Baramki, 2010); deportations of faculty and administration (Baramki, 2010); governmental surveillance (Zureik et al., 2011); refusal of permits and licenses (Baramki, 2010); military raids of campuses (Ashrawi, 1996; Baramki 2010); forced closures (Baramki, 2010); financial harassment (Al-Haq, 2015), denial of foreign faculty visas (Rahman, 2009); suppression of research (Amit, 2015), and even incursion of armed forces on campuses (Global Coalition to Protect Education from Attack, 2018; Jebril, 2018; Palestine News Network, 2018). Many of these challenges can arise suddenly, creating uniquely chaotic and uncertain environments in which to operate educational institutions.

Theoretical Grounding

Education is not a neutral enterprise. Structures, policies, and curricula emerge and evolve from social negotiations between stakeholders with differential quality and quantity of social power (Apple, 2019). This section sets the case study in concentric theoretical landscapes, first in the direct, immediate environment of occupation, which is then couched in settler colonialism, which is then couched in larger, globalized phenomena.

The Israeli occupation and colonial settlement project is asserted and advanced through robust infrastructures and tools that extend Israeli control of land and people (Berda, 2018; Halper, 2000; Weisman, 2007; Zureik et al., 2011). *Occupation* is not merely the presence of Israeli soldiers, but the politico-military machinery comprised of armed forces in combination with restricted roads, checkpoints, separation walls, travel permits, bureaucracies, regulations, prisons, sniper towers, economic controls, development licenses, bulldozers, and more. In other words, Israel's occupation of the West Bank is not merely military but is significantly instantiated in a matrix of Israeli infrastructures that crisscross the landscape and underground. Easterling's (2014) concept of infrastructure space as a set of material types of infrastructure (cables, pipelines, waves, routes, gateways, etc.) provides a conceptual basis for exploring mechanisms by which Israeli entities control the flow of global resources in and out of Palestine in ways that impact the Palestinian higher education sector. The concept clarifies ways infrastructure conditions collective behavior in subtle, yet powerful ways. In other words, infrastructure and bureaucracy mitigate the need for direct force. In addition, the work of Weizman (2007) and others (Meiton, 2019; Peteet, 2017; Zureik et al., 2011) on the exercise of dominance through geo-spatial and bureaucratic mechanisms provide vocabulary for exploring the tools of occupation that influence access of Palestinian higher education to global and internal ideoscapes and financescapes.

One of the defining features of the Palestinian experience over the last 70 years has been the progressive dispossession of land. Veracini's (2006, 2010, 2013) work around settler colonialism frames the socio-political relationship between the Israeli occupation and settlement project on the one hand and the Palestinian community on the other. Veracini is part of a larger scholarship addressing settler colonialism theoretically (Wolfe, 2006) and in the Palestinian context (Halper, 2021; Jamal, 2017; Lloyd, 2012). Veracini (2010) defined settler colonialism as the systematic replacement of an Indigenous population with a colonial civilian population, what Veracini termed *transfer*. In contrast to colonialism in general, in which the metropole dominates a new territory for the purpose of extracting economic value, settler colonialism is about expropriating the land itself and pushing out current inhabitants. Veracini theorized that settlers, in pursuing the moral authority to enact these transfers, seek to maximize their status along two spectra: indigeneity and righteousness. Thus, settler groups seek to increase their claim to being Indigenous while decreasing rival claims. Settler colonial groups rationalize expropriation based on being Indigenous and deserving.

Settler colonialism is a conflict between communities, competing for the same land, each with their own narratives and discourses. Thus, settler colonialism ignites and sustains ideological and demographic struggle, not merely armed conflict. The literature identifying the erasure of Palestinian history and memory (Benvenisti, 2000; Khalidi, 2006; Shehadeh, 2008) resonated with Veracini (2010) on this point. The literature attending to intellectualism in Palestine also suggests social awareness of the national importance of education (Atshan, 2019; Said, 1994). In this multidimensional physical and conceptual space, transfer of communities from/to land is executed. Tactics of transfer, again from Veracini, include necropolitical transfer (military liquidation), ethnic deportation, conceptual displacement (in which Palestinians are reframed more generically as Arabs, thus deprived of their specific Indigenous claim to Palestine), perception transfer (the presence of Indigenous communities are left out of the frame of reference; as in the historical narrative that Jewish immigrants settled an unoccupied desert), administrative transfer (redrawing administrative and municipal boundaries and the rights attendant with citizenship in these zones), settler indigenization (in which settlers are reframed as Indigenous), and narrative transfer (where the Indigenous society is reframed as hopelessly backward or immorally brutal). I use settler colonial theory to suggest ways PCUs as well as faculty and administrators engage with these discourses.

Socio-political contexts undoubtedly influence the structure, character, and effectiveness of higher education systems. Colleges in politically unstable, territorially contested, and occupied regions operate in especially turbulent contexts (Bose, 2010; Turner & Hoba, 2015), facing unusual challenges.

Colonial powers tend to approach education as a strategic political function to socialize successive generations of inhabitants (Veracini, 2010). Colonial instruction may aim at political indoctrination, religious conversion, acculturation, or the technical preparation of inhabitants for certain roles in the colonial regime. In this context, the withholding of educational options may also be considered politically strategic. Education in a settler colonial context has also been studied. The literature around American Indian boarding schools is a case in point (Adams, 2020). In contrast to some of this literature, the present study attends to *Indigenously initiated* education in a present-day settler colonial context. Although a few institutions of the Palestinian higher education system have transnational origins—a university founded by the Catholic church (Bethlehem University) and a university co-founded by educationalists in the

United States (Arab American University in Jenin)—the overall character, origin, and leadership of the higher education system is Palestinian.

Higher education stakeholders—ministry officials, administrators, faculty, parents, students, and others—bring various interests into their social negotiations, bidding for changes that suit competing or overlapping social needs. In the case of Palestinian higher education, this theater of negotiation is subjected to the processes and outcomes of a dominating Israeli theater of social interests to which it has been subjected through the mechanism of the occupation. This overriding theater is comprised by social negotiations across Israeli society with direct or indirect impact on Israeli policies toward Palestine.

Higher education systems operate in transnational contexts as well. Appadurai's (1996) conceptual work around scapes and disjunctures is helpful in describing the global, dynamic context within which the complex relationships between Israel and Palestine are situated. In Appadurai's work, ideoscapes, financescapes, ethnoscapes ebb and flow across international borders, continually reconfiguring relationships between regions and populations. Connection to various scapes and flows yields benefits to populations. Thus, the positioning of an economy or nation in relationship to a given scape is rendered a core interest of the state. Israeli interests behind its structures of occupation and settlement come into sharper focus considering this framework.

The Israeli occupation and the settler colonial project undoubtedly impinge on the higher education system on national, regional, institutional, and individual levels. Likewise, actors from each of these levels pursue a range of goals in response to and despite these challenges. The splintering of Palestinian administered territory into isolated enclaves likely affects basic functions of PCUs, including admissions, research, purchasing, and strategic planning. Furthermore, the separation of the West Bank from Gaza presents its own challenges. How do these complex and overlapping geographies, bureaucracies, and histories affect the coordination of higher education as a coherent national sector? Little is known in international academic literature about the potential impact of settlements on Palestinian higher education, whether through direct tension with settlers, land seizures, increased physical proximity, or the introduction of settlement universities. As the occupation affects faculty and student lives, it may result in loss of learning (Inter-Agency Network for Education in Emergencies, 2013; Sperlinger, 2015) and generate deeply disorienting logistical uncertainties (Global Coalition to Protect Education from Attack, 2018). The potential global dimensions of the Palestinian academy are mitigated by enforced isolation, limiting the flow of academic resources within and beyond the Occupied Palestinian Territories (Global Coalition to Protect Education from Attack, 2018; Sharabati-Shahin & Thiruchelvam, 2013). Thus, the discourses and infrastructure of the settler colonial occupation carry epistemological force with which Palestinians Academy must recon in pursuit of Palestinian aims.

Higher education is a site of contact between neoliberal, critical, settler colonial, and decolonizing energies. Ethnic studies scholar la paperson (2017) suggested a framework for analyzing these energies. Per la paperson, the *first university* is neoliberal, brand based, and capitalistic. The second university is *critical, liberal, and romantic*. The third university is *revolutionary, decolonizing, and resourceful*. The fourth university refers to knowledge production that occurs apart from formal higher education structures, in families, community groups, religious groups, and so on. La paperson's third university is not located in a particular department, but rather operates wherever in the institution a decolonizing energy exists and begins to assemble resources for action, wherever individuals find each other, bring the resources at their disposal together and begin creating what la paperson called decolonizing assemblages. This study uses la paperson's framework in a slightly modified form as a tool for analyzing the presence of neoliberal, normalizing, settler colonial, liberal, traditional, and decolonizing energies as they exist and operate across educational structures.

Research Questions

The research questions for this study are the following:

RQ1 How do faculty and administrators working at Palestinian colleges and universities in Bethlehem perceive the occupation to affect their students, their institutions, and their work?

RQ2 How do faculty and administrators working at Palestinian colleges and universities in Bethlehem describe their adaptive efforts to create and sustain meaningful educational opportunities for students and pursue their research, given the unique challenges of life in Palestine?

This study will be of interest to scholars of modern Palestine, peace and conflict studies, and international higher education as well as educators and policy makers working in these areas. Although this project will be most properly about the Palestinian context, scholars and educators of/in other settler colonial contexts may also find transferable insights.

Methodology

Using the methodological approach of a regional case study provided the opportunity to focus on higher education in Palestine and consider the geography, policy, and culture around and within the universities. This approach was designed to illuminate the role and function of the higher education system in a complex context. The tools for data collection included conducting semi-structured interviews with university members; collecting artifacts such as photos, campus newspapers, accreditation documents, and syllabi; and writing observational field notes from site visits. This article is from a larger study about higher education in the whole West Bank (including East Jerusalem). This article presents a subset of results from Bethlehem, which is inside the West Bank and immediately to the south of Jerusalem. Because the current structure of the higher education system emerged from the Oslo process, the temporal boundaries for this case study are the present day and recent past, back to the 1990s. This study was approved by an institutional review board.

Case Study as Method

Case study is a flexible method of research that allows for intensive study of one case in its natural context. Its flexibility is in the space case study affords for using multiple relevant types of data to reinforce and support findings. A given case study might include combinations of interview data, focus group, artifacts gathered from case sites, documents, archival material, or direct observations. I use case study because it is a flexible enough approach to allow for deeper exploration, more detail, more nuance, more interconnections within the "case" and between the case and its context than many other forms of qualitative or quantitative research with more rigid restrictions. It lends itself to a naturalistic approach, which means it allows for learning about the topic in the places where it is naturally situated as opposed to removing the phenomenon to the physical sterility of a lab or the disembodiment of a study (Flyvbjerg, 2006). A case study approach is also good for working with multiple participant perspectives on the same issue, allowing the research to "acknowledge multiple realities having multiple meanings, with findings that are observer dependent" (Yin, 2014, p. 17). This capacity to study in a relativist mode is important for studying groups or events that are controversial or contested, such as those in Palestine.

This is a *regional* case study, which simply means the case is defined by a geographical area and includes relevant phenomena inside the area, higher education in Bethlehem in this case. Using a regional case study method allowed me to focus on higher education in Bethlehem and consider the geography, policy, and culture around and within the universities. This approach is designed to illuminate the role and function of the higher education system in the complex, settler-colonial context of Palestine. The tools for data collection included conducting semi-structured interviews with university members and collecting artifacts such as photos, campus newspapers, accreditation documents, and syllabi.

Data Collection

I conducted research trips in June 2019 and March 2022 to the West Bank to explore basic institutions, geography, conduct interviews and focus groups, and gather physical artifacts and documents for review. These trips also allowed me the opportunity to observe campus spaces, both interior and exterior layouts, and location of campuses in their larger urban contexts. I toured inside buildings and between buildings on campus at three institutions in Bethlehem: Bethlehem Bible College, Bethlehem University, and Dar Al-Kalima University. I was also able to observe physical infrastructures of the Israeli occupation such as checkpoints, the separation barrier, and military facilities. I noted of areas where Palestinian campuses and physical manifestations of the Israeli occupation were proximate, on the hypothesis that the proximities would bear on the lived experience of individuals (Palestinian students, faculty, and administrators) and on systemic issues at the institutional level. While in Palestine, I established relationships with faculty and administrators of higher education institutions in Nablus, Birzeit, Bethlehem, and Hebron as well. These contacts provided insight to the study, provided introductions to colleagues, and some of those in Bethlehem have become participants in the study. For purposes of this article, I focused on institutions and their associated personnel in Bethlehem.

Given the research questions, which explore experiences and perspectives of individuals as actors (not merely as witnesses), the study included interviews as a central form of data. The interviews in this study are designed "not to measure, predict, or classify" participants, but to help understand them (Josselson, 2013, p. viii). I developed a protocol document to guide these semi-structured interviews to facilitate a flexible exploration of participants' experiences, aspirations, and activities vis a vis their roles as faculty, staff, and administrators. I asked participants about their experiences in higher education, their perspectives on how the occupation affects higher education functions, and how they respond to these challenges as they pursue their responsibilities. As semi-structured interviews, these primary questions served to guide the interviews broadly, but provided flexibility to follow up as additional areas of interest emerged.

Initially, invitations to participate were placed on public platforms where Palestinian academics participate. To protect participant confidentiality, I created an encrypted online form in which those interested in participating could register their information and designate how they would like to be contacted. Given the travel restrictions during the COVID-19 pandemic, I was unable to travel to Palestine during the interview phase, so I conducted 60- to 90-minute interviews with participants on a secure online platform between February and June, 2021. As participants were identified, I sought additional participants through chain-referral sampling. My goal was to interview up to five employees from each institution. I was able to interview between four and seven participants from three institutions for this study—a total of 16 individuals. I held a single interview with 13 participants and two or more interviews with three participants. Interviewees included one president, a vice president of academics, a dean of students, a dean of an academic program, 5 director level administrators, and 9 faculty members (see Table 3). Many administrators served their institutions as faculty members as well. In

Table 3

Participants in the Study by Institution

Institutions	Participant Position
#1	3 Deans
	1 Cabinet-level administrator
	1 Faculty
	2 Staff leaders
	8 Students
#2	5 Faculty
	2 Cabinet-level administrators
#3	3 Faculty
	2 Deans
	3 Staff leaders
	20 Students

addition to the employees, I held focus groups with 8 students at one institution and 15 students at another institution.

I audio recorded the interviews and focus groups and submitted these recordings for transcription which produced text documents with verbatim representations of the discussions. I lightly cleaned the transcripts, removing the rote researcher statements at the beginning and end, false starts, and other non-substantive material, and uploaded these transcripts to a qualitative research platform (Dedoose) for close reading and analysis.

I also continually collected documentary evidence to enrich and triangulate with interview and direct observation data. These documents included material referenced by interviewees and subsequently collected from them, screenshots of social media activity from individuals and institutions, system-level documents from the Palestinian Ministry of Higher Education and Scientific Research, and books and other documents written by participants or other Palestinian faculty or administrators (Table 4). I procured and read the Israeli dual use restrictions, a document that contains information about materials and supplies that Israel prohibits from importation into the West Bank and looked for supplies and materials that colleges and universities might use for normal functions. These interviews, along with documentary evidence and direct observations, offered a rich dataset about these institutions and the individuals who work in academics and administration. Although documents were collected throughout the study process, particularly if participants referenced and submitted documents during interviews, I also collected a large corpus of documents during and following the 11 days Israel bombed Gaza between May 10 and 21, 2021. The documents in this set include screenshots of

Table 4

Documentary Evidence Reviewed for the Study

Documentary data included:	Quantity
Social media posts and pages (individuals)	25
Social media posts and pages (institutions)	19
Images submitted by participants	23
Books authored by participants	3
Articles, news pieces	4
Ministry reports	2
Dual use restrictions document	1

social media posts from Palestinian students, faculty, administrators, and institutional accounts of colleges and universities. These posts included text, picture, and video content. I also collected online articles from news sources in the United States, Europe, Israel, and Palestine regarding the events leading up to and including the bombing. I uploaded all documentary evidence to our qualitative analysis software, along with the interview transcriptions for coding.

Data Analysis

I approached the coding process as cyclical in nature and "organized chronologically, reviewed repeatedly, and continually coded" (Creswell, 2003, p. 203). I began coding after I conducted four interviews and coded cumulatively as the project proceeded. Codes primarily arose from the data using emic categories, emerging from the substance of participant interviews, documents, and direct observations, but I also included a few codes based on etic categories drawn from literature on settler colonialism and higher education in conflicted regions. These etic codes included *infrastructure, occupation, knowledge production, Palestinian identity,* and *land.* Because "topic-based nouns do not tell you as much about the human condition as verbs, gerunds, and the participants own words" (Saldaña, 2017, p. 78), I opted to code the interview transcripts with in vivo, process, and values codes. In subsequent rounds of coding, I used pattern analysis (discerning trends and themes) to develop findings from the data (Saldaña, 2017; Yin, 2009).

I also analyzed the documentary data. Based on the insight that documents are social products that "reflect the interests and perspectives of their authors" (Saldaña & Omasta, 2018, p. 69), I approached the documents as another layer of data that could suggest, nuance, and enrich findings. I used values coding to construct an understanding of the identity of the authors and curators (Saldaña & Omasta, 2018). Because "visual analysis is a tacit, intuitive process" (Saldaña, 2017, p. 83), I noted my first impressions as well as subsequent observations when working with images.

I generated frequent field notes during my research trips. I often added field notes multiple times a day, after each meeting to capture observations, insights, and other cognitions while they were at the clearest. My field notes also include notes taken after observing contextual elements and individuals on the street, from the car or bus, passing through checkpoints, driving on the roads, going on tours, and so on. These field notes, along with the pictures I took on my trip I also uploaded to our database and analysis platform for coding and processing.

Trustworthiness

In pursuit of an approach to research credibility that is appropriate to qualitative inquiry, Lincoln and Guba (1985) suggested four criteria: *credibility, transferability, dependability,* and *confirmability.* The following section is about the first of these criteria. Maxwell (2013) defined validity, which is closely connected to credibility, as "the correctness or credibility of a description, conclusion, explanation, interpretation, or other sort of account" (p. 121). Qualitative research presents a host of potential ways for the validity of the inquiry or conclusion to come into question. I discuss the *validity threats* that are salient to this project and the measures and evidence I gathered to mitigate these threats.

Conducting research in a culture different from my own culture is complex and can be fraught with hermeneutical and interpretive risks. Kvale and Brinkmann (2009) stressed the difficulty in discerning "the multitude of cultural factors that affect the relationship" (p. 144) of researcher to participants. If research is conducted in a language that is not the primary language for either researcher or participants, then these risks are even larger. I conducted interviews in English, which is not the first language for participants. Additionally, modern Palestinian culture is complex, expressed in communities in the Occupied Palestinian Territories, Israel proper, and in global diaspora, with recent history under a parade of colonial powers, various shades of religious and secular, urban and rural, globally connected and isolated, with a wide range in levels of education. My own cultural context is also complex, with the multiple identities that influence my positions within my communities and the larger world. Conducting research across such complexity, the potential for miscommunication, under-communication, or unoriginal communication in this study was real.

I am also cognizant about some of my own subjectivities relative to this study. The possible effects of these subjectivities in this study are multivalent, ranging from my identity as White, American, male, with advanced degrees, with ready access to filtered media accounts, Christian faith identity, with commitments to social justice, and previous connections to Palestinians. These subjectivities influenced what data seemed relevant or noteworthy to me during analysis and subsequently, what data shaped the findings (Maxwell, 2013). In seeking to address these credibility issues, I agreed that "validity threats are made implausible by *evidence*, not methods; methods are only a way of getting evidence that can help you rule out these threats" (Maxwell, 2013, p. 121). To follow up on Maxwell's point, I describe measures I put in place to nurture the credibility of the research process and conclusions, and the evidence these measures yielded.

Although participants' primary language is Arabic, they have typically received formal education in English. Many Palestinian faculty and administrators, having obtained their advanced degrees internationally, have also lived and studied in English language contexts and have experience with detailed conversations in English. I also read a translanguaging statement at the beginning of each interview, inviting participants to use Arabic language words and phrases at any point in the interview. This statement was intended to give space for participants to use words and phrases that best suited their intended meaning, and on a few occasions, participants availed themselves of the opportunity. In these cases, participants used Arabic words and constructions to express themselves. We then discussed how they would approximate the meaning in English, using as many English words as needed to expand on nuances. During later analysis, I also referred to other sources for definitions to complement those of the participants.

To resist chance associations and effects associated with given data types, I also sought to triangulate the analysis across multiple forms of data. When interview transcripts, direct observation, and documentary evidence all supported a conclusion, I could hold the conclusion with greater confidence. This multilayered research design allowed data types to build on, reinforce, and complexify the findings. To make these structures plain, I sought to make the connections between the conclusions and data types explicit in our discussion. The multiple positions articulated by participants with different roles and from different institutions also provided triangulation of perspective, generating avenues to search for and address discrepant cases (i.e., examples that go against the presuppositions of the study or against the overall trajectory of the findings). By seeking disconfirming perspectives, I sought to ensure the study reflects the complexity endemic to any human context and reduces a tendency to confirm my personal inclinations as a researcher. To enhance accountability, I sent interview transcripts to participants for review in a process called member checking. Researcher subjectivities cannot be eliminated, but they can be made explicit (Maxwell, 2013). Based on this point, I describe my positionality in the next section on the role of the researcher. I also sought to develop substantial, specific, and transparent accounts of the research process.

Role of the Researcher

I am a fourth-year PhD student in the higher education department at a university in California, USA. The research described in this article is part of my dissertation work. I have worked for 16 years in higher education in the United States, having held non-tenure track faculty and administrator roles at colleges in the Southeast and Midwest. Cross-cultural research can be beneficial, but also comes with limitations and even pitfalls regarding perspective and interpretation. There is no singular perspective. Although the dominant paradigms help create categories in the literature, they cannot be applied bluntly to peoples and societies. On an academic level, I approach Palestine as a settler colonial context characterized by an asymmetric relationship between Israel and Palestine. I am persuaded that cognitive justice is a necessary pre-condition of social justice, that the freedom for local and regional communities to hold and synthesize knowledge in their own ways is essential (Santos, 2014). This idea animates much of the work represented in this article.

As a practicing Christian, I am culturally proximate to Christian faith groups that view the modern state of Israel as a divine fulfillment of Biblical prophecy and have constructed and disseminated theological teachings that explain and justify the settler colonial system as God ordained. This Christian Zionism has tended to erase Palestine and Palestinians. One of my underlying personal motivations for conducting this study is to challenge this erasure and to help my community to see Palestine, which has been, for us, hidden in Israel's shadow.

My identity as a Christian may create religious links with Palestinian Christians—links characterized by shared familiarity with religious stories, teachings, and vocabulary—that I do not share with secular or Muslim Palestinians. I was cognizant of this identity at different times during the study while interviewing participants from multiple religious backgrounds. This study began in the last years of the Trump presidency, which also made my American national identity salient in relationship to Palestinians. When the United States moved its embassy to Jerusalem and then advanced the "Peace to Prosperity" plan for Israel, it highlighted for Palestinians that the United States is unfriendly toward their interests. Although this development did not seem to affect my relationships with the participants, I cannot know how these events might have affected my credibility with prospective participants who opted against joining the study, and it became another mental burden born by our participants. I perceive being a student has had multivalent effects on my relationship to participants, some of whom are motivated to help out a student, but others of whom may have chosen to not participate in the study out of perceptions about the credibility of a student project. Cultural and geographic distance may not have always been a hinderance to the project: I have had some conversations with participants who seem to have been happy to "speak one's heart to someone not a part of one's life—someone to whom one can disclose without consequences" (Josselson, 2013, p. 5).

These dimensions of my identity as a scholar cannot be neutralized in pursuit of a vision of unbiased research, nor should they be. Rather than seeking to achieve epistemological *neutrality*, which I do not believe is possible (Saldaña & Omasa, 2018), I sought to be *transparent* instead. By being self-reflective and sharing transparently about my identity and values and how they relate to my research questions, approach, participants, and findings, readers have the tools they need to translate the findings for their own purposes. With Kvale and Brinkmann (2009), I affirm that qualitative study is "intersubjective and social, involving interviewer and interviewee as co-constructors of knowledge" (p. 18). Readers can also participate in the co-construction of knowledge by seriously considering how the process and findings of this study translate to their own lives, understandings, and practices.

Findings

Profiles of Three Institutions

There are multiple institutions of higher education in Bethlehem that have classification with the Ministry of Higher Education & Scientific Research as well including Palestine Ahliya University and Caritas Hospital College of Nursing, but this study focuses on three institutions: Bethlehem University, Dar Al Kalima University, and Bethlehem Bible College.

Bethlehem Bible College

An interdenominational group of Palestinian Christians led by Bishara Awad founded Bethlehem Bible College (BBC) in 1979. Awad, recently returned to Palestine from his collegiate education in the United States, wanted to help encourage Palestinian Christians to remain in Palestine instead of emigrating. He determined that a Palestinian bible college would help. Awad was principal of Hope Christian School in Beit Jala (a neighboring village to Bethlehem)—this school served as BBC's first physical campus. In the 1990s, the college moved to its current location on Hebron Road, a facility previously used by the Helen Keller Home for the Blind (Figure 32). In 2007, BBC founded a sister institution in northern Israel to serve Arabic-speaking Israeli Christian populations. This institution later merged with a seminary and became Nazareth Evangelical College. Awad served at president of BBC until 2012 when the current president, Dr. Jack Sara was inaugurated. According to the institutional website, BBC exists as "a Palestinian Christian evangelical university college that works in the service of, with, and through the Palestinian community, and aims to prepare potential leaders in Palestine and the world and participate in promoting a Palestinian Christian theology

Figure 32

Bishara Awad Center at Bethlehem Bible College, Bethlehem, Palestine. Picture Taken by Author

locally and internationally" (BBC website). In 2021, BBC claimed 81 actively enrolled students at the Bethlehem campus and 48 employees, six of whom are academic teaching staff (Ministry of Higher Education and Scientific Research, 2021).

The college offers BA and MA programs in biblical studies, peace studies, ministry, and tourism. The college is accredited by the Middle East Association for Theological Education, the Palestinian Ministry of Higher Education and Scientific Research, and other agencies. BBC now also runs a satellite program, largely virtually, in the Gaza Strip. The college plans and hosts a popular conference called Christ at the Checkpoint, a conference designed to engage the worldwide evangelical community in theological discussions about the oppression of the Israeli occupation. BBC is governed by a board of seven local trustees, including a human rights lawyer, ministry leaders, business professionals, and higher education leaders. BBC is classified by the Ministry of Higher Education & Scientific Research as a University College. Students tend to come from the Bethlehem area, nearby areas in the West Bank, Hebron, and East Jerusalem.

Students used to enroll from Gaza, but Israeli policies now prevent students from Gaza from attending.

Bethlehem University

Bethlehem University (BU) was founded in 1973 by the De La Salle Brothers, a catholic fellowship dedicated to running education centers around the world. The De La Salle Brothers had been running a school for boys on the same location in Bethlehem since the 1890s. In 1973, the school moved to a new location and left the campus facility for the next university (Figure 33). The BU website points to Pope Paul VI's 1964 visit to Bethlehem, and his subsequent desire to do something to bless the Palestinians, as an impetus for BU's founding. As of 2022, the university claims more than 3,000 currently enrolled students and 17,282 alumni (website citation). The mission statement on the BU website says BU "is a Catholic co-educational institution in the Lasallian tradition whose mission is to provide quality higher education to the people of Palestine and to serve them in its role as a center for the advancement, sharing and use of knowledge" (website reference). BU is classified by the Ministry of Higher Education & Scientific Research as a traditional university. The university is a member of multiple associations, including the Palestinian Council of Higher Education, the International Association of Universities, and the Association of Arab Universities. BU has an international board of regents and a local board of trustees. In 2020-2021, BU reported 504 employees, of which 260 are academic teaching staff (Ministry of Higher Education and Scientific Research, 2021). Of the teaching staff, 97 hold a doctorate, and the rest hold a master's degree (Ministry of Higher Education and Scientific Research, 2021). The university has faculties of arts, science, education, business administration, hotel management, and nursing and offers

Figure 33

Bethlehem University, Main Entrance to Millennium Hall. Picture by the Author

multiple undergraduate degrees in each faculty and graduate degrees in a few of the faculties (website citation). Figures 34–37 show other parts of BU's campus.

Figure 34

Bethlehem University Memorials to Student Martyrs. Picture by the Author

Figure 35

Bethlehem University Chapel of the Divine Child. Picture by the Author

Figure 36

Plaque of Donors to the Bethlehem University Library Renovation. Picture by the Author

Figure 37

Bethlehem University Main Entrance, Missile Hole Visible on Second Story of the Library. Picture by the Author

Note: The main entrance to Bethlehem University. The circle can be seen on the second floor of the library where an Israeli missile pierced the stone and destroyed part of the building.

Dar Al-Kalima University

Dar Al-Kalima (DAK) was established as a university college in 2006 as the first institution in Palestine to focus exclusively on the arts and cultural heritage (Figure 38). The incoming class was 22 students in the first year. As of 2021, Dar Al-Kalima University is classified as a traditional university by the Ministry of Higher Education &

Scientific Research. It was a university college until the administration restructured and successfully applied for an upgrade in status in 2020–2021. There were 510 students actively enrolled at Dar Al-Kalima in 2020–2021 and 115 employees including 60 academic teaching staff (Ministry of Higher Education and Scientific Research, 2021). Of the teaching staff, 43 have graduate degrees. Since Dar Al-Kalima is an arts university, some of the master's level degrees may be terminal degrees. According to the institution's website, Dar Al-Kalima exists to "To build a country, stone by stone; to empower a community, person by person; to create institutions that give life in abundance" (DAK website). DAK is governed by a board of directors. To pursue this mission, the institution pursues goals such as offering unique programs in arts-related fields and to contribute to the cultural richness and renewal of Palestine (Figure 39). The university offers arts and culture degrees in areas such as performance, film, graphic design, jewelry design, art and antiquity preservation, culinary arts, and tourism studies.

Figure 38

Main Plaza at Dar Al Kalima University Picture by the Author

Figure 39

Mosaic and Artifact Restoration Laboratory. Picture by the Author

DAK runs a satellite program in Gaza as well. DAK runs a small publishing house as well that publishes books by DAK faculty as well as other Palestinian cultural leaders and researchers.

Multiple themes emerged from the analysis, centering around challenges the Israeli occupation presents to Palestinian higher education at individual and institutional levels and adaptive Palestinian responses that allow the continued pursuit of education and learning goals. Findings are presented in the following categories: (a) challenges to individuals and institutions, (b) faculty and administrator aspirations and goals for students, and (c) individual and institutional maneuvers to overcome the challenges.

Theme 1: Challenges

Participants described a wide range of challenges students face including physical, psychological, economic, academic, and spiritual as they reflected on the higher educational system and the role of the occupation (Table 5). For the most part, participants connected these challenges to the occupation, but also pointed to challenges arising from students' families, from their colleges, and from Palestinian society.

Admissions

In addition to impacting individuals, checkpoints impact colleges at an institutional level. One of the major implications of checkpoints and the resultant reduction in mobility between cities is an increasingly local proportion of the student body and, in some cases, shrinking enrollments. One participant described the logistical issue: "Our college is also shrinking in numbers and why is that? Because of the most people who can come from Ramallah to [name of college], they need about an hour and a half a day going and another hour and a half a day back. We're talking about three good hours to and from Bethlehem." Without the detours and checkpoints, it would be a 25-minute commute. In the case of colleges and universities in Bethlehem, they are not only near major checkpoints that govern entry and exit from Bethlehem and its environs, but the Israeli built separation wall also zigs and zags across the northern and western edges of town, geographically fragmenting collegiate markets. From the perspective of prospective students, these mechanisms of the occupation tend to constrict college choice to the few local options that may be available. Alternatively, families who can afford rent for their child may consider making the difficult choice of sending their student to live in another city so they can avoid daily commutes through checkpoints.

Table 5

Code Frequencies: Theme 1: Employee Perceptions for Student Challenges

Codes	Example Quote	n
Checkpoints/separation wall	"Students who commute from Jerusalem and Hebron, they have to go through checkpoints and the predictability of how long it will take them -- they could just go through a checkpoint quickly or they could be stopped and searched and undergo security checks and that could take we have no idea for how long."	29
Economic opportunities	"Because of the sort of the economic situation in general, Palestine suffers which means students can't afford education and the universities are under resourced."	26
Gaza	"We do have a number of online students from Gaza. And obviously, the challenge there is that although they are in Gaza, an hour and a half drive, they can never come to Bethlehem. Another challenge that they are facing, they always tell us we do not have electricity. You know, we barely can live. We barely can eat."	14
Israeli soldiers	"If somebody has killed somebody or they know somebody who's a relative or a neighbor [who is killed], that affects them psychologically a lot."	14
Instability	"What we usually say is that the unpredictability of things here in terms of being able to access checkpoint and being able to go through it every day, the ability to get a visa or to get a permit, not knowing what might happen, this whole sense of unpredictability, we find it to be quite taxing not only for students, even for us."	8
Admin. detention/ arrest/house arrest	"We have a student who was detained for several months and that affected his studies tremendously."	7
Demonstrations	"The college is situated in a unique position next to a checkpoint so demonstrations are not alien to us. Often, every Friday, there are demonstrations that happen and surely, these young students have questions about what to do and what not to do."	6
Home demolition	"Her building [home] was destroyed by the Israeli army in the last 3 months. So, our students and our staff, they're living in fear and anxiety what's gonna happen tomorrow."	6
Land appropriation/ settlements	"I have a student this year from [name of town] where Israel now is building one of the biggest settlements around Bethlehem and trying actually to evacuate parts of [name of town]— it's very close to my student's family—in order to enlarge the settlement."	8

Dreams of Emigrating

Participants also discussed the connection between the challenges of living in the West Bank and some students' dreams to emigrate out of Palestine. When asked how many of their students leave, participants said very few have the economic means to emigrate. One participant estimated that around 10% of her students could leave if they tried, and then a smaller percentage do. Another, from a different institution mused that up to 30% of her students emigrate. Regardless of the institution, participants want their students to be "hopeful and rooted, not to give up on our land."

Many students dream of a better life elsewhere. Although the majority will not have the opportunity to leave, some encounter these opportunities, and many of these do decide to leave Palestine, often to the larger oil economies in the region.

> Our society in general is influenced by being under occupation, which means there is a sense of hopelessness. There is a sense of young people thinking that the best option we have is to leave. There is a sense of always feeling powerless and not able to change things because we have been subdued as a society, as a nation.

This institutional leader is pointing to the effect many of the challenges described above has on students. These challenges contribute to a widespread desire to emigrate, to get away from the pressure and difficulties. Another participant talked about the contrast between the student's perceptions of the outside world rooted in YouTube videos and their personal experiences of living under occupation. For this participant, the wide gap between the world visible on YouTube and personal experience created an unbearable and unrealistic wish for something better among students. Indeed, when asked to raise their hands if they would like to move away from the West Bank, most students (roughly 80%–90%) raised their hands in all the focus groups run for this study.

Participants also talked at length about unemployment rates. Multiple participants talked about the trade imbalance with Israel, that Palestinians import a large proportion of what they consume from Israel and are unable to export products to offset the deficit. Participants generally perceive these economic challenges to also stem from the occupation and connect them to the widespread unemployment in the West Bank as well. The economy in Bethlehem is centered around religious tourism, so the COVID-19 related lockdowns have been uniquely difficult. For many of the students in this study, lack of job opportunities commensurate to a college degree is part of their desire to emigrate.

Procurement/Purchasing

The dual use list includes a range of materials, supplies, and equipment that can occasionally or frequently be used in higher education settings for teaching or research. These include seeds, chemicals, advanced computing and engineering equipment, fertilizers, certain metals, lathes, mills, remote control technology, telescopes, GPS technology, and casting furnaces. When asked, participants shared stories about materials or supplies they need for classes, but they cannot receive. Items mentioned by participants included seeds for their biology faculty, chemicals for cleaning in the Jewelry Design program, chemicals for developing film for a photography program, and components for a robotics course. In describing how attempts to procure supplies proceeds, participants talked about placing an order online or requesting permission from the Israeli authorities to import a certain product. When the request is rejected, in many cases they would go without the material. In these cases, multiple participants used the term "theoretical education" to describe the education they would offer their students in lieu of practicing with actual materials. Instead of developing film with the photography students, the professor simply describes the process to his students. In one case, a participant described acquiring seeds for their biology faculty when he was overseas and carrying them back to the West Bank in his suitcase.

Although books are not included on the dual use list, many faculty members described ordering printed materials to be shipped into the West Bank, but they never received these materials. In fact, one of the participating institutions has developed a "suitcase ministry" by which international travelers are invited to purchase and carry books needed for the library and for individual researchers with them when they travel to the West Bank.

Theme 2: Faculty and Administrator Aspirations for Students

When asked about their aspirations for their students, participants described a range of goals including the development of personal character, identity, and commitments to action (Table 6). They tended to talk about the kind of people they want their students to become (character), the self-understanding they want their students to cultivate (identity), and the kinds of things they want graduates to do with their lives (commitments). Participants seem to understand the elements within each of these areas as deeply interconnected to each other and contextually situated in relation to the occupation and other dimensions of modern Palestinian life.

Table 6

Code Frequencies: Theme 2: Faculty and Administrator Aspirations for Students

Code	Example Quote	n
Aspirations for Character		
Integrity	"What we are hoping for our students is to be people of integrity. To have integrity. The character that reflects the Christian faith and values. What I mean by that is not fundamentalist, but more open minded, loving, caring people. To be for justice and seeking peace."	8
Empowered	"Being independent, they can be entrepreneurs. They can learn how to manage their own work or hopes or ideas."	7
Critical thinkers	"I would hope that they would be a leader of some sort. I really want to create people who are not just simply screws in the machine, but people who can think for themselves."	5
Aspirations for Identity		
Pluralism	"We try all sorts of things to create a student body that's tolerant of others through a program that we have in religious studies all students have to take and they learn both about Christianity and Islam and where they learn to be more understanding of one another."	15
Identification with the land	"Our curriculum is quite contextual. There's a huge difference between a curriculum set in the west and another set in a college like ours in the east. We relate what we study to our context. That makes a difference, what are we learning about our history and how can we, for example, implement that in our day-to-day life living in the land of the Bible."	14
Student identity	"Arabic is our Native language. It's our mother tongue, and they're [the students] Palestinians. We were all born in Palestine, our parents, our grandparents, so this is our land. This is where we belong"	12
Global citizenship/cosmopolitanism	"That is really what I feel is the biggest contribution that I gave to [name of institution], another international perspective from someone who understands the culture and who can bring in all of these outside ideas, repackage them in a way that doesn't sound shocking or obtrusive or disruptive to the system that we are in."	7
Aspirations for Student Commitments		
Commitment to stay in the land	"We want them [the students] to be rooted in Palestine like an olive tree with deep roots, with all the history and so on, and yet having their branches widespread into the world, so to have their grounding in the Palestinian Arab society, and yet to have a dynamic understanding of this identity with open doors and windows to the world and to keep that balance."	18

Code	Example Quote	n
Sacrificial service	"We talk a lot about volunteering, about giving, not always taking. We send them into mission trips. We send them into different activities."	14
Leadership	"We have students and our main goal or our main vision is for these leaders to serve in their own community. We do not see, or at least I do not see, my students graduating and serving in America or other countries. The harvest is plenty and the doers are few in our country."	9
Resisting victimhood	"Instead of crying and being passive, we want you [the students] to give yourself the permission to do things, you know, despite things. It might help them to survive. It's starting to believe that the occupation isn't permanent. Better to show that you are giving yourself the permission to do things despite anything else."	7
Resistance	"So, as the follower of Jesus, you know, I think there is an obligation to proclaim truth to power, you know, to write about it, to demonstrate peacefully, to engage in nonviolent resistance, you know, in all of its forms. You know, this is for me part and parcel of our gospel expression, of our gospel proclamation."	5

Nurturing Strong Character

When reflecting on the values and characteristics they seek to cultivate in their students, participants talked about hope, empowerment, and integrity. As one senior leader put it:

> First of all, our hope and our aim is that they will not run away from their problems. They will not run away physically, meaning emigrating, but also, they will not run away psychologically, meaning becoming fundamentalists or become depressed and feel it's hopeless or they will not think that violence is the answer. […] we are trying to train our students not to fall into these traps because these are easy traps around everyone, but how to face the situation with creativity and how to find ways to deal with the challenge so that the challenge will not occupy our students, but that our students be in control of the situation.

This participant sees their students struggle to stay motivated given the challenges they face, but they want their students to be hopeful and creative people.

The hope and sense of agency participants seek to nurture in their students serve a critical counterbalance to the challenges they face, not just the physical and economic control of the occupation, but the struggle against hopelessness. Several participants also reflected on their desire to see students grow in their sense of integrity. They see this as both an immediate need, reflected in their discussions about plagiarism in college, and as a long-term need, reflected in their discussions about corruption and the need for future Palestinian leaders to pursue national interests over personal interests.

Nurturing Palestinian Identity

Participants also described their hope for students to grow in their sense of identity as Palestinians, as Arabs, and as global citizens. Multiple participants observed that their students are spatially or directionally unaware and cannot articulate their location in relationship to the land of Palestine. An art instructor explained, "Some of them were like they never realized directions, I mean as simple as that […] Because one of the things in such a context is happening that people get—They lose feelings of space, of time, of direction, you know." Participants seek to nurture a greater familiarity and connection with the land among their students:

> It's a struggle for many of our Palestinian students to really be grounded in their identity, so we like to remind them that they are Arab Palestinian Christians, and of course, they're Arab because they speak Arabic. Arabic is our Native language. It's our mother tongue, and they're Palestinians. We were all born in Palestine,

our parents, our grandparents, so this is our land. This is where we belong, but of course, we should not separate our Christian identity from that too.

This professor seeks to overcome the challenges students face in developing their own attachments to Palestine.

Participants also expressed that they hope students resist internalizing an identity of being victims. Participants connected this to an assessment that Palestinians often are known as victims, and less commonly known for their innovators, artists, engineers, and other culturally constructive practitioners. They want something different for their students. "I mean, instead of crying and being passive in a way, it's more you [the student] give yourself the permission to do things." Practitioners try to promote these positive identities for their students in their classes and through mentoring.

Nurturing Student Commitments

Participants expressed that they want their students to pursue certain aims in their lives. More than any other goal, participants said they wanted their students to stay in Palestine, to not emigrate. In addition, they want their students to sacrificially serve their communities, to take up leadership, and to resist the Israeli occupation.

One of the most pronounced themes in these interviews is that professors and administrators at these institutions wish to see their students make their future lives in Palestine, to become sacrificial leaders for the future of Palestine. Participants described these aspirations more than any other aspirations for their students, including that they become critical thinkers, that they resist the occupation, or that they find a job: "Absolutely. As [name of their college] seeks to train locally, I would ultimately want to see them in this land where Christianity first started. I think it's such a shame to see our students leave especially considering the small minority of Christians that have remained in this part of the world." When asked to share about students who have gone on to fulfill their professors' hopes, participants shared stories of students who have stayed in Palestine while fulfilling positions in which they could serve their society as educators, artists, entrepreneurs, clergy, and other such roles, even if this meant passing up opportunities for a greater quality of life outside of Palestine. As a professor of business articulated:

> I want to see our graduates to love this land and to stay in this land and to stick to this land and do whatever they can to develop a decent life on this land. To me, this is very important because this is part of our mission. We need to develop the Palestinian people and develop the Palestinian economy.

This professor highlighted the economy as a contested space where these struggles are also played out. Many of those interviewed expressed that they empathize with their students' desires to find a better life outside of Palestine, and they continue supporting their students' choices even if they emigrate.

Theme 3: Maneuvers to Overcome the Challenges

Although participants were happy to talk about the challenges their students face and their aspirations for their students to thrive despite the occupation, they were plainly passionate about the practical ways they seek to help their students (Table 7). Palestinian educators and institutions represented in this study seek to actualize their aspiration for students in the face of challenges from the occupation by (a) cultivating safe havens in which to learn, (b) mentoring students for wholistic health, and (c) nurturing student attachment to the land.

Table 7

Code Frequencies: Theme 3: Adaptive Structures and Practices

Code	Example Quote	n
Offer educational programing	That's why I mentioned earlier that we created an incubator, for example, a business incubator. That's a new idea where we push students to start businesses, small businesses that grow over time rather than keep on seeking job opportunity and employment at a certain institution.	21
Teach and mentor	I started personally doing mentoring to 5 students or I may try to make at least once or twice a semester. And many of my colleagues are trying to do the same	21
Ensure emotional and physical safety	What we always tell our students is that once you step into [name of institution], what we want to is protect an environment that is safe, that's predictable, and that this would be a normal way of life rather than being always under harassment or uncertainty.	21
Nurture attachment to the land	"I take them out to Area C to paint. And just connect them more to the place. Not to the metaphysics of the place. It's more to the reality of the place. To the ground itself."	14
Offer online programs	"The vision of the online program came out of necessity and not out of luxury. In the other parts of the world e-Learning is let's say a luxury. You could travel to Los Angeles if you wanted, but, you have family obligations, so you do it online. But in Bethlehem, if you want to reach people outside of Bethlehem, we do not have any option but to do it online."	14
Set academic standards	"My standards are high, and I expect students to live up to them, and they do. The thing about Palestinian students is that despite the weak high school system, they get really smart. They really manage to turn around."	11
Cultivate learning environment	"We make an educational environment for our students not where they feel worried and anxious about what's going to happen, but to feel relaxed, to feel that they have a space to learn, to be impacted, and to excel so they could in the future hopefully be like that for other people."	5

Building Safe Havens to Learn

Participants talked about how important it was to them to make their campuses safe and peaceful havens from the uncertainties of the region. Many participants expressed concern for student safety and emotional health. Student safety often came up close on the heels of conversations about checkpoints, demonstrations, and settlers. Safety is also connected to the unpredictability of life in the West Bank, especially in East Jerusalem, Area C, and certain parts of Hebron. These conversations frequently included conversations about how they wanted campus to be predictable, beautiful, or peaceful places. One administrator talked about how important it is for their campus to provide opportunities for restfulness:

> The unpredictability of things here in terms of being able to access checkpoint and being able to go through it every day, the ability to get a visa or to get a permit, not knowing what might happen, this whole sense of unpredictability, we find it to be quite taxing not only for students, even for us. What we always tell our students is that once you step into [name of campus], what we want is to protect an environment that is safe, that's predictable, and that this would be a normal way of life rather than being always under harassment or uncertainty.

This sentiment, the desire to offer a physically and emotionally safe environment came up across all the institutions in the study. Another administrator at one of the other institutions, which is located near a major checkpoint where Palestinians sometimes congregate for political demonstrations against Israel, demonstrations where Israeli soldiers have been known to release tear gas and shoot rubber bullets, explained that when they know ahead of time that a demonstration is planned, they will often send out text messages to their students and meet for class in a church building further away from campus to teach and learn in a quiet and uninterrupted space. Occupation related factors are not the only stressors from which students escape when on campus—students at one institution spoke about the pressures of family expectations on them. Some of them described families whose elders put pressure on them to certain professions or to act in certain, sometimes more culturally traditional ways, and these expectations create stress when at home. Campuses have become places for these students to make new relationships, engage across gender lines, and get some distance from the weight of family expectations.

Mentoring for Wholistic Health

Several participants from different institutions spoke at length about how they view themselves as more than teachers of content. They approach their students, who have needs that span intellectual, mental health, and spiritual, as mentors and even "friends" as one participant put it. These participants talked about "Opening our hearts and doors for them [the students] in many ways." The same participant went on to share about one student:

> One of my students, she's struggling a lot psychologically. You know, she's been through trauma, and it's been impacting her. And what we're trying to do, how we could minimize the anxiety that she is having without losing her academic work. So, I think we're trying to make education for our students not where they feel worried, you know, and anxious what's gonna happen, but to feel relaxed, to feel that they have a space to learn, to be impacted, and to excel so they could in the future hopefully be like that for other people.

As is evident in this quote, these professors and institutional leaders expressed personal care for their students' lives, not only for their academic performance. One professor of spiritual formation described her conviction that she should actively practice her faith-based value of loving her enemies when she was passing through checkpoints and this became a practice in which she mentored her students:

> As a teacher, I never pretended to be courageous or that I could do things that they [the students] could not do but I made sure that I had to be very genuine in what I shared with them and very real because as a Palestinian Christian, I also struggle with such things. From my own personal life, I would always ask God for strength to love even as I go through checkpoints and to be Jesus to people who are trying to persecute me or to humiliate us.

This professor encourages her students to observe similar, faith-based practices.

Nurturing Student Attachment to the Land

Participants also expressed their desire that students stay in Palestine to build a life and contribute to society. Individuals and institutions executed a range of actions that they think of as promoting this outcome among their students. While acknowledging students will still seek to emigrate and that it is their right and understandable to do so, these faculty and administrators sought to help their students stay and thrive in Palestine. To connect their students more deeply to the land of Palestine, to help them develop familiarity and emotional bonds to the land, they incorporated field trips and other experiences outside the classroom. One art professor expressed it this way (this professor referenced Area C, which is the zone in the West Bank in which Israel exercises full military control and in which Israeli settlements are being built):

> One of the things we're trying to do through the course is to take them out and paint outside. We go to different areas, to Area C. We connect them more to the place. Not to the metaphysic of the place. It's more to the reality of the place. To the ground. And then often many of them, they started more and more going out, you know, and practicing their place. And looking at different things. Even walking in nature. Walking in their place despite everything, despite the restrictions. Because one of the things in such a context is that people lose feelings of space, of time, of direction. I used to say "Let's go to a village nearby. It's only 6 kilometers away from where they live. But they feel the distance exaggerated so much. This is because of the occupation, but then they started to go, and they are building a better relation and more understanding of even their surroundings.

In a similar vein, a professor of history explained:

> If we go to a place, you can see a couple of historical layers, different eras. This landscape is the ultimate landscape. We see olive trees because during the Ottoman times, they wanted people to cultivate their land to pay taxes. So, trying to enlighten them and get them looking at the ground—And one of the things I noticed that many of them started to look at their surrounding in a new way. Looking at their villages. Trying to think about the history of the place in a different way and realize we are inside layers of history.

In addition to using programs and experiences to promote affective bonds to the land, participants spoke about strategic offerings designed to give students the skills they would need to earn a living in the challenging economy of the West Bank. Institutions in

Bethlehem offer certificates and degrees in programs such as tourism leadership, medicine, engineering, education, and business. One dean spoke at length about the entrepreneurship incubator at his institution designed to help students launch their own businesses. In other words, many—not all—participants connected conversations about job readiness directly to the goal of helping students secure their ability to remain rooted in the West Bank.

Emphasis is on cultivating a spirit of service to society in collegiate experience. One professor who takes her students to neighboring countries to serve Syrian refugees spoke passionately and at length about how her students perceive themselves as "victims because they've been under occupation for so many years" but after this experience they "just change completely, dramatically in a positive way." This professor reflected that the students who are transformed through these experiences "start thinking there is something I need to do here."

Profiles and Portraits

In this section, I present anonymized, composite portraits of individuals to suggest ways some of the themes might be expressed in context. I change names and combine aspects of multiple participants for the sake of both conciseness and anonymity.

Lara

Lara, a senior leader at her institution, teaches occasional classes in addition to her administrative duties. She is passionate about the institution where she works and to help equip her students to be servant-hearted leaders in Palestine and critical thinkers. She attended Birzeit University for her undergraduate education, a university north of Ramallah, at a time in the early 1980s that she considers to have been a kind of golden age of intellectual life and political resistance on campus. She remembers taking courses with Hanan Ashrawi and remembers fondly the grassroots spirit that was present among the students, staff, and faculty at the time. She is concerned her current students are not meeting and building relationships with Palestinians from other parts of the West Bank and Gaza. Due in part to the checkpoints, they do not travel as often to other areas, and there are fewer students enrolling at her institution from outside of Bethlehem and surrounding areas. A few years ago, she took her students on a field trip to a neighboring Palestinian town and realized from their comments that they think of the town as a foreign space. She sees this fracturing of Palestinian space and society as a significant problem she seeks to address in whatever ways she can. Lara spends much of her time in meetings and completing paperwork for the Palestinian Ministry of Higher Education and Scientific Research. She is also involved with helping her colleagues write syllabi and design academic programs for her institution. Lara also knows many of the students at the institution and divides her time between her various duties and encouraging the students. Some of her colleagues need supplies or equipment that are hard to procure. Israeli authorities prohibit importing a whole range of resources her faculty need for their classes. Photography faculty cannot get darkroom chemicals. Jewelry faculty cannot buy chemicals needed for cleaning metal. Her biology faculty need seeds for their lab that Israel prohibits. Lara tries to help in different ways, either to obtain the needed materials or to help her faculty manage without them. Lara lives in East Jerusalem, near the old city. As a result, according to Israeli administrative law, she has to maintain her *center of life* in Jerusalem or she risks losing her residency there. She also commutes each day through a checkpoint to get to and from work in Bethlehem. The length of the lines to get through are unpredictable. As an executive leader at her institution, she contributes to strategic decision-making across enrollment, curriculum, personnel, and finance. She is concerned at the lack of quality employment opportunities for her graduates and seeks to provide educational opportunities and formational experiences that will open professional doors for her students.

Elias

Elias is a senior professor at his institution and teaches a full load of courses each semester. He is well regarded by his students and colleagues. As a Palestinian citizen of Israel, he attended college in Israel, but then spent several years in Germany and England earning his Master's and Doctoral degrees. After graduate school, he accepted a position as an assistant professor at a university in the United States where he worked for several years before returning to Israel. He commutes from his house in Haifa each day to work at his institution, which means he passes through a checkpoint coming and going. He looks for opportunities to spend time with his students outside of class, to get to know them and encourage them as they grow. Elias is concerned about his students. He worries that they have a lot of growing to do before they can be successful adults. He thinks they need to learn to apply themselves with greater effort and focus, to think more critically about their world, and to commit themselves to higher levels of integrity. After his academic training in parts of the world that emphasize the importance of original academic work, having students who copy and paste work to satisfy assignments bothers him. He likes to emphasize academic standards of excellence with his students and challenge them to stretch their capacity. Elias is one of only a few professors at his institution who is active as a researcher and writer. He has authored multiple books with reputable academic publishers from Europe. He also writes and publishes articles regularly for journalistic and popular outlets. He encourages his colleagues to be active researchers and writers as well.

Taima

Taima is studying to be an interior designer. She aspires to graduate from her institution in Bethlehem and then get accepted to a graduate program in Europe. She lives with her family in a small village between Bethlehem and Hebron, which means she commutes past Israeli settlements, roads where Israeli settlers drive, and Israeli soldiers each day. Her mother and father, her brothers, and her grandparents are supportive of her decision to go to college, but they do not appreciate some of the ideas she is starting to pick up from her studies and from fellow students. When she is on campus, she spends time in mixed gender groups and meets Christian students and faculty, which she does not think is noteworthy, but which concern her family. Last year, Israeli soldiers and workers demolished her friend's house in a nearby village, and her friend's family moved away north. Her friend had to unenroll from the university and transfer to a university closer to where she moved. Taima has not been to Jerusalem, a 15-minute drive from where she goes to college, since her family brought her when she was very young. As a resident of the West Bank, she needs special permission from the Israeli authorities to visit Jerusalem. If she ever has the chance, she dreams of emigrating away from the West Bank and establishing life elsewhere. Paris sounds nice. She is on the university soccer team, and in fact, has played for the Palestinian national team in her age bracket as well. Taima has cousins who live in nearby villages who do not have access to the Internet. In fact, sometimes the electricity to their village is inconsistent or gets cut off.

Wasim

Wasim is studying computer science and technology. Because Israel restricts the import and use of remote-control technology in the West Bank, he had to learn some of his robotics courses from a book even though his professor wanted to build projects with the students in the tech lab. Wasim's family is from Bethlehem, where he lives with them. He is also athletic and aspires to establish an athletic club in Bethlehem after he graduates. Wasim appreciates the business classes he takes at his institution as well—he feels they give him a slightly better chance at his dream to be an entrepreneur. Last year, when Wasim traveled to Jerusalem with friends for the holiday, an Israeli soldier put the barrel of her gun in his face and yelled at him. When he shared this story, Wasim did not worry too much about it—he said he was used to it. When asked where he was from, he did not say Bethlehem. He shared the name of the village where his family lived before the state of Israel was established, where they fled from in the 1948 war. Wasim has not seen one of his friends from the university for a few months because Israeli authorities placed him under house arrest after he participated in political demonstrations in Jerusalem. Sometimes Wasim finds it hard to concentrate on his coursework due to stress he feels many days. He often opts to spend a lot of time with his friends and family instead.

Discussion

The story of higher education in Bethlehem is broad and complex, taking in the challenges, aspirations, and practices of Palestinian educators and students from multiple institutions in the enclave. Students, faculty, and administrators—coming from around the region, from Bethlehem proper, from Hebron to the south, from Area C, and from

East Jerusalem—bring their diverse experiences and identities into the sphere of locations, norms, and practices associated with their higher education roles. Other forces are also part of the story, including the Ministry of Higher Education and Scientific Research, the governance structure under which these PCUs operate, and the matrix of Israeli occupation practices and infrastructures are also part of the story of higher education in Bethlehem. The religious identities of the communities who share Bethlehem, particularly Christian and Muslim communities, also bring unique and multivalent identities into view.

Palestinian faculty and administrators in Bethlehem see the unique challenges their students face. Indeed, they face the same challenges themselves: high unemployment and the danger and hopelessness for an Indigenous society that can be connected to life in a colonized and occupied place. Yet, they nurture aspirations for their students to thrive in Palestine, to contribute to the ongoing maintenance of a healthy society, to raise their families, and to sacrificially serve their neighbors. To help their students toward these aspirations, faculty and administrators engage in a range of actions, including making campus life safe and predictable, mentoring students, and taking students out, away from campus to nurture familiarity and connection to the land.

Veracini (2006, 2010) viewed settler colonialism as defined by the systematic *transfer* of an Indigenous population out of the land and the transfer of a colonial civilian population into the land. According to Veracini (2010), transfer is perpetrated through a range of tactics including conceptual displacement (in which Palestinians are reframed more generically as Arabs, thus deprived of their specific Indigenous claim to Palestine), perception transfer (the presence of Indigenous communities are left out of the frame of reference; as in the historical narrative that Jewish immigrants settled an unoccupied desert), and narrative transfer (where the Indigenous society is reframed as hopelessly backward or immorally brutal). Evidence from this study is suggestive that another tactic can be added to Veracini's list: the creation of physically, economically, and emotionally uncomfortable conditions for indigenes that incentivize "voluntary" emigration. This study also provides specific evidence that Palestinian higher education is a site for specific resistance to these tactics. For example, educational programs designed to create positive encounters for Palestinian students with their own land; faculty who help students explore and inhabit their identity as Palestinians, and institutions that provide opportunities to students to prepare for culturally diverse roles in society. Although PCUs may also be sites where neoliberalism, factional competition, and clientistic politics are exercised, the evidence from this study indicates they nevertheless remain sites for resisting Israeli settler colonialism as well.

This study does not provide a basis for describing Palestinian higher education in other parts of Palestine (e.g., Hebron, Birzeit, Nablus, and Gaza City). Further research could also elucidate the unique challenges to higher education arising from the different configurations of occupational infrastructure. For example, Al Quds University has four campuses, each located on different sides of borders and separation walls, whereas Hebron Polytechnic University is located in a city where there are urban Israeli settlements. Further research would be required to understand the influence of proximate occupation infrastructures to campuses.

CHAPTER 5

CONCLUSION

Some stories are about land, so much so that the land functions as a sort of character. In the United States, stories about the frontier function this way. Daniel Boone and Davy Crocket explored the untamed frontier and leading settlers to new lands over mountains and across rivers. The land is both a source of danger and of life in these stories. There are a lot of these stories that are part of American mythology—Land myths, Little House on the Prairie, Paul Bunyan, Lewis and Clark, and John Henry. The fact that some of these stories are based on historical figures is mostly beside the point: The stories *function* to depict a certain relationship of certain people to the land, a relationship of destiny, inevitability, and even moral rightness. Certain strains of Christian Zionism advance spatial stories as well. They portray a certain relationship between particular people and particular land.

Discussion

The land discourse in my Christian Zionist community pushes our Palestinian brethren into the shadows. But there is another Christianity, another form, practiced and lived out, expressed in some of the institutions in this study that does something different: It sheds light on the Palestinian situation. It liberates. In Chapter 2, I explored my faith-based connections to Christian Zionist ideas. It was in my church where I was enlisted to send gifts to the Israeli embassy. I also absorbed spatial stories about Israel from Christian books and movies. The theology that drove these stories makes no room for Palestinians in the land of their birth. This version of Christianity fostered a theological vision that both dissolved the connection of Palestinians to their land and, to some degree, overlooked their existence altogether.

Participants in this study work and study at three institutions in Bethlehem, each of which are Christian institutions in their own ways. Although this means they are not representative of other institutions in the West Bank in some ways, they do offer insight into the ways Christians are living in the village where Jesus was born and the ways Christian faith can inform higher education in uncertain environments. In contrast to the Christianity in my background, they represent forms of Christianity that do not bind or pass over Palestinians, but rather liberate them. They even nurture theological resources that provide religious energy for such liberation, such as an anti-imperial theology, a theology for those under oppression from a foreign government. Jesus of Bethlehem turned out to be different from the Jesus with whom I grew up.

Spatial Machinery and Mind

Spatial machinery is a metaphor for the emergent properties of settler colonial infrastructures, policies, and practices that tend to transfer some populations in and others away. Like complex machinery, it has components that perform discrete functions: bypass roads, checkpoints, walls, etc. Different components do different things, perform different spatial jobs, such as demobilizing, sorting, separating, blocking, funneling, and containing populations. It's a little like machinery on a factory floor.

This machinery performs opposing functions depending on the population. It mobilizes certain populations and demobilizes others. It enables development for certain populations and blocks development for others. The functions these components perform can be perceived as having a few types. First, there are declared, official functions. The road is *for* conveying traffic. The checkpoint is *for* allowing authorized persons through while blocking all others. Second, there are undeclared but official functions. These might include secondary objectives for a given piece of infrastructure. Third, there are undeclared, unofficial functions. The placement of the Israeli road in the West Bank blocks further development of the Palestinian village. The checkpoint closures fragment Palestinian communities from each other. The placement of the separation barrier will increase pressure on Palestinian communities and separate them from their farms and families. These undeclared, unofficial functions are just as much a part of the spatial machine as are the other functions and, in fact, may be the more potent functions. This third type of function may also emerge more organically than the others, through adherence to unstated norms and values in planning processes and cannot necessarily be documented as the intention of leaders and planners. What emerges across the machinery is its differential functioning toward communities. Although it creates paths for one community, it blocks paths for another. Although it makes space for one community to build, it constricts space to build for another community. In this way, it is a settler colonial machine.

Spatial control entails knowledge control. Because knowledge is produced in space, controlling people's place in space impacts prospects for knowledge production. Denying Palestinians access to Jerusalem not only denies access of Palestinian bodies to travel to a physical location, but also to the range of knowledge products that come from that encounter, the memories, the access to details, the human interactions, the potential for human relationships to form, the affective knowledge that can emerge. Thus, spatial machinery has epistemic functions as well. With this spatial-epistemic machinery as a clear and present condition, Palestinian higher education performs multiple complex, sometimes conflicting functions. This study suggests Palestinian higher education can provide tools for a minority to depart from the spatial machinery of the West Bank (emigration), tools to pursue private gain in the midst of the machinery of occupation and settlement (neoliberalism), tools to fight against the occupation (resistance), and tools to contribute to Palestinian culture and society in the midst of the occupation (social investment). These functions are not all mutually exclusive—some can be pursued simultaneously or sequentially. This study highlighted various adaptive practices used by higher education institutions and individuals, practices that sometimes just help keep classes running despite threats to that happening. These practices are ultimately aimed at helping students stay in the land, make a life in Palestine, resist the oppression, and contribute to a strong and flourishing culture and society.

Epistemological Resurgence

Resurgence is a move to advance despite past or present resistance or setbacks. The idea can describe social movements, armed conflict, and other ideas. This study has highlighted another form of resurgence practiced by Palestinian educators: *Epistemological resurgence*. Younger generations of Palestinians are emerging into adulthood having grown up in a world both spatially and epistemologically controlled from outside their communities. The prospects for knowledge production are rearranged with each new wall, checkpoint, and policy that limits an otherwise freer range of experiences and associations and the knowledge that could have come from them. Palestinian educators in this study operate in this world and are aware of these dynamics, sometimes more explicitly, sometimes more implicitly. Many of their efforts could be characterized as epistemological resurgence—if the knowledge cannot be produced in *this* way, then we will produce it *that* way. If the skill cannot be taught *experientially*, then we will teach it *theoretically*. If the students are struggling with their experiences *on their own,* then we will support them to cope through *mentoring*. If the student cannot learn something *here*, then we will send them *there*. If the students *have never been to* Jericho, then *we will take them* on a field trip. And so, some Palestinian educators can be thought of as epistemological coaches, helping their students grow as epistemological agents in an epistemologically pressurized context.

What is the aim of this epistemological coaching? Evidence from this study suggests it is to provide the tools needed for Palestinians to grow as whole people, healthy, ready to lead their communities, ready to serve their communities, at peace with their neighbors, and ready to remain in the Palestinian territories or at least remain connected to Palestine. Students are enamored with the idea of life outside of the West Bank. Most of them want to leave, yet most will remain.

Implications

Revising Powerful Stories About Land

Some stories about land, maybe especially theological stories about land, are surprisingly powerful. They make claims about who belongs in the land that reinforces political and ideological positions and that affects decision-making such as voting, philanthropic giving, and educational content. This study included an autoethnographic reflection on Christian Zionism and the ways American Christians can participate in a form of theological storytelling that provides theological warrant for Israeli settlement in the Palestinian West Bank (Chapter 2). The following implications are rooted, for the most part, in those reflections. Christians should be careful about what land-related stories they tell and how they are constructed. At their worst, the stories we tell about land—whether Christian Zionist stories, Manifest Destiny stories, or otherwise—can help settler colonial machinery run under the cover of a legitimizing story. Practitioners of certain fields should be especially circumspect. Societies often give historians, archeologists, and theologians the unique power to narrate who belongs where. These stories can be advanced in many places, in academic journals and conferences, from the pulpit, through tourism, in the classroom, and in the family home, so everyone has the potential to be a storyteller, and everyone should accept that storytelling about land has consequences for others.

Tourism is an immersive form of engaging a story of a place visited. Those stories can be political, most dangerously if they do not appear to be political. Even if the story is implicit in the itinerary, it is still there. Yet, tourists not only construct a story about the place they have visited, but also empower that story by financing it with their money. By patronizing the overall destination, by selecting certain tour companies, tour guides, attractions, historic sites, and so on, tourists have a hand in shaping the narratives that are told in each place. The land itself, the destination, can be configured by spatial storytellers. Even as the storytellers remain behind the curtain, the environment itself has been turned into a text that tells an authorized story. Like visiting a Disney Theme Park, or watching the Truman Show, destinations are configured to present a story, but under the story, between the locations, there is another world. There is a practice in forestry of leaving a visual buffer strip of trees along main roads, even when clear cutting the rest of the hillside. It is a form of visual storytelling that hides a larger reality. Something similar can take place when visiting Palestine-Israel. When American Christians visit the holy land, they should go with an understanding of these implications. Those who are interested in a deeper and more wholistic understanding of the place should construct their plans critically and get off the beaten path. The stories are different in the places that are harder to find from the main roads.

Reconfiguring Relationships to Space

Space that is touched by humans is generally configured. It is shaped to perform functions. A field might be dug, a fence installed, a barn erected, a house built. These components and their arrangement are a configuration known as a farm. Individualized spaces, each locked with a door of reinforced bars, along a gallery, with a cafeteria, bathrooms, a central yard, and separate spaces for guards, and all enclosed by a high wall is a configuration known as a prison. Space can also be configured at larger scales as well. Highway systems are massive configurations that convey and direct traffic to some places (and not to others). This study included a spatial analysis of Bethlehem, Palestine, of the infrastructures of Israeli occupation and settlement, and of educational spaces in higher education (Chapter 3). The following implications are largely rooted in this analysis. To the degree that moving through space shapes prospects for knowledge production, and spaces are configured to reveal some things and hide other things, this study highlights the importance of epistemic humility—holding loosely to the perceptions that emerge from encountering space. Although the spatial machinery that Palestinians live in is unique, all people live in their own society's forms of spatial machinery, governed in many places by zoning laws that give rise to their own paths, destinations, infrastructures and the forms of knowledge that are promoted in these spatial configurations. But these machines direct traffic away from people and places that are not among the common points and routes. This reality should promote epistemic humility about the places where people live.

De Certeau (2011) used the term strategy to describe the built environment and the ways elites intended for people to inhabit those spaces; tactics to describe the sometimes surprising ways people navigated these environments. This study may highlight the value of cultivating innovative tactics. Improvising tactics could include selecting new destinations, staying longer, or leaving sooner than usual, taking a new route, using a different mode of transportation, walking, or biking instead of driving, making different choices with time, and a range of other tactics. If the connection between space and knowledge that is proposed in this study has validity, then changing these tactics will have implications for knowledge—they will nurture new stories about places and people.

Engaging With Leaders From Inside the Machinery

This study included a case study of colleges and universities in Bethlehem, Palestine, of administrators, professors, and students, and of the challenges they navigate, the educational goals they pursue, and the adaptive practices they enact as they navigate inside the spatial machinery of the West Bank. The following implications are drawn largely from that section.

The participants in this study teach, lead, study, and live in the West Bank (including East Jerusalem); thus, they have a direct and intimate knowledge of the spatial machinery in which they live. It is true that they are victimized by an oppressive machinery and the societies that build and maintain it, yet they use creative approaches to navigate, create, and overcome as well. Students want to leave the West Bank, but most will not have the means to do so. Most faculty and staff have vivid goals and strong commitments to invest themselves in the next generation. Many of these participants questioned how many allies they have from outside the machinery. They wonder if their story is being heard. They are looking for people and institutions they can trust who can partner with them in bringing their stories to new places and populations.

La paperson (2017) proposed higher education systems contain individuals, small groups, and resources that can be continually configured and reconfigured into *decolonizing assemblages*, that despite the presence of neoliberal and colonizing energies in these institutions, there are also pockets of decolonial passion. These pockets can link up in quiet, out of the way places across departments, campuses, and institutions to form what la paperson calls *the third university*. This third university is possible and can continue being nurtured, not only among colleges and universities in Bethlehem, but also across the West Bank, Gaza, and internationally.

Parting Thoughts

After completing this study, some things are clearer for me, and others are more confused. When I began this study, the primary language and concept I used to describe the Israeli policies in the West Bank was that of occupation, but this study has illustrated for me how helpful the language of settler colonialism is for describing the current situation. Israeli settlements are built throughout the West Bank, including East Jerusalem. The military occupation functions, in large part, to provide a matrix of security to support this settlement project. The occupation has been in place since 1967, but the settlement project has progressed and enlarged almost as long. Although there is a lot to say and qualify about this assessment (that Israel is advancing a settler colonial project in the West Bank), I hold the assessment as fundamentally plain and obvious after this research. What is more confused for me after this research? I am morally committed to a course of peace and peacemaking, but the relationship of peacemaking to decolonization is more problematized for me. The cessation of violence is not a sustainable peace unless systematic oppression is dismantled. Barring that dismantling, violence will break out again. But systems take time to come apart, and in the meantime, people are losing loved ones and living under unjust terms. Decolonizing can lead to an increase in conflict; whereas peacemaking, depending on what is meant, can ignore, or minimize past or ongoing oppression.

I grew up in Richfield, MN, just a few miles from where Derek Chauvin put his knee to George Floyd's neck. My family moved there in 1990—thousands of miles away, the First Intifada was over, and the Oslo Accords were yet to begin. A few years later, a West Bank family would welcome the birth of their little girl, Abir. And 10 years after that, in 2007, an Israel soldier would fire a rubber coated steel bullet that would strike Abir Aramin in the back of her head as she ran away. She was taken off of life support after a couple of days. Years later, in 2020, George Floyd would be murdered not far from my childhood home. He was murdered the year after Abir would have graduated from college. My family and I recently visited the corner of East 38th and Chicago to see the shrine in front of Cup Foods. We met a member of the Floyd family. We bowed together with George's family in a sacred moment when my son of 12 years old offered to pray for her. Although they were very different people living in very different places, George Floyd and Abir Aramin both died at the hands of security personnel. After both of their deaths, people tried to make sense of their murders by suggesting they were in the wrong place at the wrong time or that they were somehow victims of their own decisions. But that's not it. They both lived inside systems that put their families and their communities at a structural disadvantage and that brought a premature end to their lives. In a sense, they died at the hands of society.

Millenia prior to all this, a young couple welcomed a newborn baby into the world. He was born in Bethlehem, a village under occupation. The powers that be sought to murder him, but his family escaped with him to Egypt as refugees. When the immediate danger was past, they returned to Israel and lived in Nazareth where the young Jesus grew up. He would go on to a life of ministry, teachings, and sacrifice. The empire in whose spatial machine he lived would put him to death in his early 30s. He was buried in a tomb in Jerusalem in a place where most Palestinian Christians today are not allowed to go. Jesus too, was put to death at the hands of the state.

Printed in the USA
CPSIA information can be obtained
at www.ICGtesting.com
LVHW080157031223
765141LV00073B/1380

9 781640 313156